Enigmatic

Benefactors

Donald G. Brooks

Libri Agni

Summary: Enigmatic Benefactors: The life and times of 1850s London, England, and the struggles of families, both the wealthy and the poor.

Printed in the United States of America
Copyright © 2021 All rights reserved
ISBN: 978-1-937668-08-2

Dedication

A true treasure is a gift discovered. And many applications cover the landscape. I wish to address a specific case this book is predicated upon.

First, I dedicate this work to our daughter and son. The first child born to us was *Rebecca Nicole Brooks,* and almost three years later, *Brent Michael Brooks.*

Both, at nearly the same age, announced their individuality as they emerged from the cocoon of childhood. Both, at nearly the same age, took charge of their lives to go and challenge the world, leaving home.

Both have succeeded.

Their parents, Donald and Patricia, applaud them and wish them well in their time. Donald and Patricia have no possession so valuable to them as their children.

Table of Contents

Introduction

In the 1800s England was a bustling city in a booming time of industry and invention. Their navy was world-class and to be reckoned with.

The monarch, Queen Victoria, wanted the empire to pull together more closely, to become one in every sense of the word. Scotland and Ireland didn't fully agree. They were apprehensive about what England might do with them, moving them from their traditions and customs. There was one uprising after another. As well, between Ireland and Scotland, clans were continually at one another over the smallest of things such as the theft of a sheep.

In England it seemed there were three groups as well; there were those who were indeed wealthy, the poor, and those who only thought themselves wealthy.

Likewise, there were those who were royalty, climbers falling from peerage, and those who would do almost anything for a morsel of bread and a safe place to sleep. Birth, life, and death were constants. Each day brought one of the three.

Our encounter meets all three as they struggle with their unique issue, vying for solutions and happiness that seem so elusive. Each person is searching to find peace and happiness with as much as possible, a portion of sheer joy for the day.

CHAPTER I

TRIBULATION OF THE JUST AND UNJUST

The year was 1843, 35 days until Christmas. Market Court in Kensington displayed no evidence of the quickly approaching holiday. In the streets no one shared talk of festivities. London's East End was the most wretched to be found. The city stretched for 24 miles, east to west. Most, living in the squalor, were consumed with the many mouths to be fed each day, one day at a time.

Across the dirty street, from the third floor, a buxom woman leaned from of a window shouting, "Maxwell! Maxwell, you get back here right now," her voice rising with each word. "I'm not letting you run the streets like your brother. No good will come of it." He stopped and dejectedly returned, kicking up small clouds of dust as he toddled along back to his residence.

Another window opened. A young woman looked down to be sure no one was below, then threw a large pan of dirty water to the street and closed her window.

A disproportionate number of sprogs outnumbered the adults in the streets each day, plying their skills to help with needs in their homes. No crime practiced by adults was off-limits to the young. It seemed every family, including Jews, Quakers, and Gypsies, was on the take.

Few were employed and did better. Often, a family was accused of pooterism for wishing to ascend economically to a better class. However, escaping the neighborhood seemed an impossible task.

Judaism was a prevalent religion. Jews had left Russia by the thousands. Christianity was next largest. Catholicism was almost stamped out due to its expulsion years ago. In 1701 British law required monarchs to be Protestant. Few practiced Christianity or followed any faith whatsoever.

One family of the name Hamstead, including Mary and Jenkins with six of their own children and three orphans, filled to overflowing a small, third-floor flat on London's east side. The Hamsteads were good Christians in regular church attendance. An odd family to be sure, yet there was more than enough love to go around. The father was a good smithy, providing almost enough to meet their common needs, and the church, knowing their status, helped them along as they could. Their first occasion to adopt a child from the street came in 1843.

They had an idea to "save the children" by taking them out of London. In morals, ethics, and physical condition London seemed to be failing and bound for further disarray.

Mary began writing to her siblings living throughout the countryside, seeking situations and opportunities. She persisted for nearly a year, and then in the summer of 1851, they moved from London's east end to Canterbury, 40 or so miles east of London. They joined Mary's sister there for a time until they settled in an adequate, rented cottage of their own.

In a manor house 75 miles east of Piccadilly, lived Duke Henry FitzRoy VII, a descendent of Henry FitzRoy, First Duke of Grafton appointed by Charles II in the year 1675. Henry FitzRoy VII resided there with his wife, Lady Cecilia. His staff, including the household and field hands, totaled 33 and cared for the 14,350-hectare demesne which was well-situated with numerous bodies of water, much cattle, and many horses. As well, three sizeable gambrel-roofed stone barns jetted out from the hillside.

Grafton Manor, their home, was self-sufficient in most ways as it went about its daily affairs. The estate was east northeast of Dover five miles and one mile from the sea. From the disused widow's watch the Strait of Dover and the North Sea were distinctly visible along with the Foreland Lighthouse. During the summer months guests and all manner of nobility frequented their estate.

Henry's estate manager, Horton Weatherford, age 35, had served him for just over a year. He was a brawny man, strong and fair-minded. He and his wife lived in the caretaker's cottage just over a mile from the manor house.

They were of different worlds, the commoners of Market Court and the Dukedom of Henry FitzRoy.

Being without an heir at the age of 58, Henry was concerned about the continuation of his family name and estate. His family lineage was a vain matter and must be addressed as was done by those before him.

But Lord Henry struggled with a major problem. His wife's family was afflicted with hemophilia. His closest male relative was Newton FitzRoy his nephew, a fine gentleman of 24. Newton's mother, Alyssa, the sister of Lady Cecilia, was thought to carry the gene as well. So, Newton was an at-risk individual biologically and not suitable as an heir in

Henry's thoughts. He was determined to avoid the risk at all costs.

Seldom mentioned but ever-present on Lord Henry's mind was the resolution of this matter. Otherwise, Henry's position was very satisfactory. He deemed there was yet time, but time moves at a constant, leaving many affairs unfinished.

The paupers of London were not alone in their troubles. The wealthy were plagued to maintain their families, status, and estates. Each class, in its own way, struggled. Each lived with the risk of loss. Each would declare its case monumental with no sympathy toward or from the other.

Lady Cecilia and Lord Henry had married nearly 25 years earlier. His title was the Seventh Duke of Grafton, and she was the Duchess. Each understood the hemophilia matter but felt their personal devotion was sufficient to carry them through the times.

In the beginning the risk seemed light in comparison to their feelings. However, three lost children later; the picture was changed. Between the two boys was born a daughter, Victoria. She was the light in Lady Cecilia's life. She was born five years following her brother, Rudolph, and four years before the passing of her second brother, Robert.

Rudolph had passed during the chill of fall while lady Cecilia was yet pregnant with Victoria. She had considered herself blessed with the birth of Robert, having both a daughter and a son as her two surviving children. Then tragedy befell the family once more when Robert succumbed to hemophilia when Victoria was just four.

Cecilia made it her passion to care for Victoria, protecting her from everything. What was common became a compulsion.

One sunny morning Victoria, at the age of six, was permitted to walk with the farm manager, Watson, to the horse barn and back. He took his eyes from her for seconds as several horses trotted through the barn aisle just as she was entering. Several horses bolted, trying to leave, and trampled her. Watson voluntarily left their employ burdened by his guilt.

Oh, to be sure, Henry and Cecilia's love for one another was still there following such painful experiences, but the heart does not mend easily. Sometimes Henry would come upon Cecilia alone and tearful over the memories of her babies.

Even passing the children's quiet bedroom called back the grief, and she would be out of sorts for days. Other children coming around could also set her off.

On the morning of November 20th Lord Henry and Lady Cecilia were seated for a late breakfast. The housekeeper, Missus Wallander, greeted them with a curtsy as they entered the breakfast room. She followed Lady Cecilia, arranging her chair for her. "Oh, the scones look so scrumptious," Cecilia commented.

"They're just out of the oven, milady," replied Missus Wallander, pouring a brisk breakfast tea for both.

"Will there be anything else, Milady?" asked Missus Wallander as she withdrew from the table.

"That will be all, thank you," Lady Cecilia offered.

"I need to be at Piccadilly Thursday next," Lord Henry remarked. "I need to see our barrister concerning the parcel northeast of us that I'm buying. There are 267 hectares. It's very reasonable. They are asking £600. Peter has placed a retainer on it for me."

He followed closely with his offer to Cecilia. "Would you like to go as well? There are your friends to visit and an opportunity to see new fashions and Christmas gifts we will need," he prompted.

"Wouldn't it take the better part of the day to reach Piccadilly?" she asked.

"Yes," he answered.

"Then we would have to stay over. How long might that be?" she continued.

Lord Henry hadn't initially believed she would care to go, thus neglecting a thought to accommodations. He quickly improvised, "I'm thinking the Forbes House at Piccadilly would be a fine place to stay for as long as we wish. It was converted a few years ago following the death of the former owner, MP Henry Hope."

"That sounds very nice. How many days will we visit?" she continued.

"Well, how long would you like?" he questioned. "We needn't be in a rush."

"I believe I can be ready to travel by Tuesday. The day following your business affairs, we might return home?"

"Yes," he smiled in agreement and added, "And we must take care to prepare for difficult weather this time of the year."

Lord Henry reached for the bell pull. One minute later, Missus Wallander appeared.

"Yes, sir?" she asked as she arrived.

"Will you send a footman to ask Mr. Weatherford to meet me at 11 on the rear terrace?" Henry asked.

"Yes, sir," she curtsied and left.

Following the collection of his papers, he made his way to the rear of the house to meet Horton.

"You wished to see me, your lordship?" Horton asked, slightly winded by his swift trek from the barn.

"Yes, Weatherford. Next week, I wish to leave for London taking the coach. I have business to conduct. Would you see to it that it is made ready by Tuesday? I think if we depart by sun-up, we could reach Piccadilly with daylight to spare. What say you?"

"Sir, I see no signs of foul weather for a time. And if it changes while you are there, you may extend your visit accordingly," Horton commented. "I'll see the coach is in tip-top shape."

"Lady Cecilia will travel with me. She is to see friends and what new things there are since last she was in town."

Horton almost smiled when considering Lady FitzRoy loose in London with several pounds of spending money, but he was careful not to let it show. The FitzRoys would as well return home with their Christmas bounty. Each year they remembered the staff, and it was always appreciated.

"Thank you, Horton," Henry concluded and returned to his personal library to finish his paperwork for the trip.

Lord Henry was to meet Peter Fenchyl, a barrister who represented him from time to time. Peter would review the purchase of the forest and such documents required to gain possession of a deed. Peter and he were close friends from their days at Oxford.

Peter from his youth had wished to become a barrister. Later, hopefully, he might attain membership on the King's Bench. To supplement his skills he had lived one year in Beauvais, France, studying criminal modalities and inquiries under the renowned Eugene Vidocq.

For the next two days Henry spent much of the time in his private study. This was a quiet room set apart from general activities and was always locked. Considerable accounting of his business activities needed attention. This responsibility was his alone. He was pleased with the work on the Manor over the past ten years. The Manor was indeed growing in size and wealth.

But here in the quiet he was most oppressed with the need of an heir. In this regard, he was ill-prepared. He sometimes considered ideas that were outside proper channels, but they were quickly discarded.

For Cecilia, the excitement grew each day in expectation of the upcoming journey. Her two large trunks rested on the floor near the front entrance. The night before leaving. Rory, Henry's valet, laid out Henry's traveling clothing for the morrow.

When the coach and horses were brought up in the morning, the trunks would be placed on the boot at the coach's back. There they would be lashed securely to the rack with leather straps.

Missus Wallander had prepared food and drinks for the day. Food that needed a cool place was put between the trunks and the coach.

The driver, Mr. Benert, assumed his place on the front seat. The footman, Mr. Girardi, stood in a small place at the rear of the coach where he could sit. Both men wore matching heavy woolen coats, with hats and gloves.

The coach stood high above the roadbed with fold-out steps. Its large wheels made it an easy job for the two teams of Cleveland Bays to pull and ride smoothly.

When the pair came from the house, the footman assisted them into the coach before resuming his perch. The staff on duty stood in a line, waving them away as the coach lurched forward and began its extended journey.

Isinglass windows on the sides and doors kept the wind out. The coach was warm and comfortable. Its brocades and grand padding assured them of comfort. Cecilia sat close to Henry as he wrapped his massive coat around her for warmth. With her head on his shoulder, she closed her eyes and attempted to catnap.

Along the journey they read together, talked of things to do in London, and spoke about what they might do with the forest, soon to be theirs.

At length the day came to a close. Nearing the Forbes House, the evening air turned to a chill, and the sun sank below the skyline and disappeared.

CHAPTER II

CELEBRATING CHILDREN

It was six days before they returned from London. When the driver pulled the coach to the front door of the manor, there were three trunks tied at the rear. Much of the interior and top were loaded with packages. Little room for seating remained. Father Christmas would be generous this year.

All the house staff scurried to decorate for the holiday. Lady Cecilia busily edited three lists: one for extended family, one for business friends, and dinner on New Year's Eve' for royalty and peerages. Preparations were made for guests who would be staying over. Thus far, on New Year's Eve', 14 would remain for short periods of two to six days. The house was in a tizzy as the staff, down to scullery maids, was on edge.

When the house eventually cleared of guests on January 5th, Lady Cecilia assembled the staff, thanking them for all their hard work. She declared it the most remarkable New Year's dinner ever.

As her comments concluded, gifts began to flow, and the staff brimmed with enthusiasm warming relationships in the house. For the balance of the day, everyone was excused, except for the most significant.

For the rest of winter, the weather wasn't so hurtful. Very little snow fell, and temperatures were unseasonably pleasant.

Fieldmen began to busy themselves, finishing work left from the fall. The little work was welcomed, a respite from the boredom of winter.

On a very bitter cold and rainy day in early February, Henry sat in the drawing-room thinking. At the door stood Maximillian Brewster, the butler. In his uniform he was a striking and imposing man. He stood over six feet tall, every ounce muscled and capable. He had been in the employ of Henry for more than ten years.

"Sir, Mr. Weatherford wishes to speak with you concerning a personal matter," Maximillian advised and then waited for a response.

Henry glanced at his papers on the tea table in front of him and responded, "Yes, that will be fine. Ask him to join me here."

With a military-like spin on his heel, Maximillian turned about and left to retrieve Horton.

The two appeared once more, whereupon Henry welcomed Mr. Weatherford.

"I've intended to speak with you. This is convenient. First, what may I do for you?" asked Henry.

"Thank you, your lordship," began Horton, "Come March, I would like a few personal days. My sister's family wishes to visit Tillie and me."

Henry reflected quietly for only a moment before a soft smile came over his face.

"I see," he said as his smile widened. "That sounds wonderful. Nothing more important than family."

Would a week off suit you better?" Henry continued. "I know we will be preparing fields soon, and if you find us in a bind, perhaps you could step in."

"Very much so, sir. I would be very willing to help should it be needed. I will advise you when we expect them, several weeks afore time, so you will be aware.

They're a very Christian family, but there are several, ten to be exact. They manage a foster home for needy children in Canterbury. Several churches in the area support them."

Horton, pausing his loquacious enthusiasm, after a moment more added, "They'll be no trouble to you, sir."

"I should like to meet them at some point, if I may," Henry encouraged. "And on to my opportunity. The additional ground I secured poses a question. What shall I do with it? Nothing should lay idle. I'm sure you agree," Henry remarked.

"I do indeed, Sir."

The new grounds lie contiguously with the northeast portion of the manor. We saw it together; you know whereof I speak. As a fellow man of the land, I believe you may have ideas.

"As some say, your lordship, you've caught me somewhat flatfooted for a response. But knowing your feelings, I will give it my attention," Horton remarked.

"Oh, and as you go, I want to say how pleased I am with your assistance. I hope the feeling is mutual. You're a valued employee," Lord Henry reiterated as Horton stood, bowed ever so slightly, and retired from the room.

Horton and Tillie wasted no time sending a letter to his sister Mary in Canterbury. This was uncommon. A whole week was something to be excited about.

Horton sent word to Lord FitzRoy; his family would visit the third week of March. Lord FitzRoy, though personally enthused about the visit, was reticent to tell Cecilia.

March 15th arrived along with the hoard of children. Cecilia's unease grew as the family paraded past the main house toward the Weatherford's home. She quietly exclaimed, "There are so many." True to form, she had to excuse herself, returning after some time, eyes reddened.

Lord Henry consoled her. "They will be staying a week or less. We must remember the Weatherfords are an important part of Grafton Manor."

Though difficult for Cecilia, it seemed not to be troublesome for Lord FitzRoy. The thought of so many children on the grounds brought a smile to his face and a sense of joy to his heart.

The door knocker at the front sounded. No one was expected, but Maximillian was quick to respond. Opening the massive, hand-carved door, he greeted Lady Alyssa

FitzRoy. Her ostentatious coach rested behind four matched horses on the horseshoe driveway.

"Greetings," he said, "Won't you please come in. Are you seeking Lady Cecilia?"

"Why, yes," she replied. "Is Cee-Cee at home?"

"Yes," he affirmed, "I will tell her you are calling," indicating she should remain in the foyer. He closed the door and went to tell Cecilia that her sister was waiting.

The two sisters greeted one another with many kisses and handholding.

"It's been so long, perhaps three years since we last visited. It was mother's funeral, I believe," Cecilia remarked, shaking her head with a tinge of sadness.

Small talk continued for several minutes before Cecilia asked that tea and biscuits be sent in.

Sensing there was a reason for her visit, Cecilia asked, "You've come all this way. Is there a special need with which I can help you?"

"Well, yes, I do have a concern I thought we could discuss. In the course of time and changes that come, we need to address them. You know," Alyssa suggested indelicately.

"Of course," Cecilia acknowledged, "What is it?"

"Well, it has to do with the future of Grafton Manor. So far as I know, Henry hasn't chosen an heir yet. He is nearing 60, and it concerns me. Now, I know it is not my business, but I wondered if I may have a solution for him."

"Yes, it has concerned us as well. Do you have someone in mind?" Cecilia inquired.

"Well, knowing his first concern, that his heir be a FitzRoy, I'd like to recommend my boy, Newton. He is quite accomplished, as you know. He's no longer the boy you knew. He is now 24 and a junior professor at Oxford," she recited to Cecilia. "And about to marry," she pressed further.

We all wish Henry many more years, so I am only thinking ahead, you see. It's been on my mind for a year now,"

"Henry and I have discussed the matter, many times. I'm very fond of Newton. You know that. But, Henry's concern remains about the ailment. He wishes to stop it in our time. Does Newton suffer from it?"

"That's just it; he rarely does. It's thought men can't give it to their offspring," Alyssa assured her sister.

"You know how I have suffered the results. Henry is doing what he feels is best. Truthfully, I somewhat agree with him, but I will take it up with him. I don't believe he will change his mind, but I will bring it up once more. It is so difficult. You do see that, don't you?"

They continued recalling family events of recent years. Cecilia didn't invite Alyssa to stay for supper, and so after two hours, Alyssa left.

As happy as the Weatherfords were to see their family arrive, adjusting their routine was a chaotic accommodation of nearly a dozen additional people, mostly little ones, meal arrangements, and bedding down the guests. The loft would be filled that night.

One by one each child was identified to the Weatherfords with his or her particular accomplishments noted. There was Mollie, age two, pretty-as-a-picture; Willard, age five, an angry-looking boy; Genevieve, age six, quiet and withdrawn; and Malina, age seven, sweet with flowing silky blond hair. The next three children were boys: August was quiet and studious at 10. Peter was tall and thin as a bean pole. Rupert was gentle and loving, a twin to Peter, both 12.

The adopted children included Laddie, age 12, a ginger-headed, somewhat thin boy; Thomas, age 15, a nearly full-grown child and a bully; and finally, Elizabeth, age 11, a stout girl with a pretty face.

The Hamstead's birth children were troubled. Yet they understood their parents' attempts to care for these homeless children; they were indeed learning patience.

Laddie, following the death of his mother, was the sullen one of the adopted children. His mother, Aggie McCallister, was said to prostitute herself to live. One morning she was found near death on the steps of St. Andrews by the Wardrobe on Queen Victoria Street. She awaited their opening, Laddie by her side, to seek food for the two of them. The Hamsteads took them in, but she died of influenza shortly thereafter.

Laddie remained. They chose to give him their name, making him a Hamstead. They thought Laddie was born September 21, 1839, near Grafton, south of Birmingham. That was according to his mother. They knew little more about him.

At every opportunity, Laddie was quick to tell of his rich parents who would someday come for him. Much of it was his imagination they were convinced. Other children often offered similar stories, knowing little if anything of their histories.

But it was clear Laddie remembered something of a past privileged lifestyle. His unusual demeanor supported his story. He enjoyed good habits and was articulate. He was kind, caring, and gentle with all. It seemed clear he would search for his family when he reached adulthood. It was always uppermost on his mind.

With great clarity he recalled sitting beside his mother and feeling lost and alone at her death. The scene visited him frequently in the night.

Five years earlier, Thomas's parents had died in a fire that burned 11 houses. Thomas was angry and exhibited that anger through his tendency to bully other children.

Elizabeth was inclined to be mean, taunting the others when she didn't get her way. No one knew her background. She was found on the street, alone one day. Elizabeth was quick to cry and be bratty, although no one could figure out how it came to be. On the surface she was a precocious child.

Mary's children and Laddie had some schooling. Only Rupert and Laddie anticipated upward mobility in the years to come. Rupert wished to become a barrister. Laddie desired to join the navy and captain his own ship.

On Tuesday Lord FitzRoy wished to visit the Weatherfords. Henry wanted to see how they got along, and he was quite fond of children in general. Their interactions with one another interested him, and he wanted to know more about them. He sent word to inquire of a convenient time to meet them.

"A morning visit might not show well," Tillie told Horton. Late afternoon the next day was agreed upon, and an answer sent back to Lord FitzRoy.

That next morning heads were scrubbed, bathing accomplished, and each child's finest clothing laid out. Only after a lunch of broth and bread were the children allowed to don their Sunday best. Following, they were seated in the shade of a large Maple near the house to await Lord FitzRoy.

While the children were busy, Jenkins asked Horton to walk with him to the horse barn.

"You have a good situation here," Jenkins offered. "I envy you," he said as he smiled understandingly. The reason I wanted to speak with you is that we struggle. We truly love the children, but we wonder if you and Tillie might take on the two older boys and Elizabeth."

Horton's eyes widened with surprise. "Your meaning is that we take them to raise?"

"Well, it's more like finishing their raising. They're good children and never give us a minute of trouble. The boys are mostly educated. They need training, a trade. And what better place than Grafton Manor. You'd never regret it."

"But, Jenkins, I don't have the authority to hire or fire," he interjected.

"I understand that, but you have influence with Henry. Both boys are strong and healthy. Elizabeth will be a fine maid. In fact the boys can do a man's work and work for just board and keep for a time," Jenkins pressed.

Already these past several weeks Horton felt he had stretched his relationship with the FitzRoys. It couldn't continue.

"Well, I'll think about it," Horton replied. "I know you understand the risk to my position and what losing it would mean."

"Oh, I do, I do. I wouldn't ask, but we have 11 mouths to feed. You have two. You're a good man, one who could put the finishing touches on the pair and assure Elizabeth a position for life. If it weren't so, I'd never have approached you."

They had drifted from the barn to the paddock, stopping to gaze at the Lipizzaner stallion.

"Was ever there a horse with more grace!" remarked Horton leaning against the stall wall. "Know what I'd like? A time to ride him. We'd go to the forest and explore. Just to be astride that animal would make me feel rich."

The children showed signs of fussiness by the time Lord Henry arrived at half-past two. He had walked from the main house on his own. Cecilia was noticeably absent.

Horton turned his attention to the fidgeting gaggle of children instructing them collectively, "Children, please stand now and each one tell his or her name and age to Lord FitzRoy as you are presented."

As Henry approached, one by one each child attempted a slight bow or curtsy before announcing his or her name and age. Laddie in particular stretched up awkwardly as tall as he could manage before his stiff bow. The elder boys suppressed the instinct to mock his shameless airs.

Following, Lord FitzRoy commented, "You're a handsome bunch. I'm more pleased than I can tell you. In you is the promise of our tomorrow. At half past three would you all like to visit the main house and enjoy a dish of ice crème?"

Exuberance broke out as they all agreed they would.

"Horton, I shall tell Missus Wallander to expect you all at that time. Is that agreeable?"

"Indeed, Lord FitzRoy," replied Horton as the children continued to express their joy.

Horton again addressed the children, "We shall walk to the house in 10 minutes. Anyone who dirties their clothing may not go, so stay looking your best."

Lord FitzRoy instructed, "And Horton, please saddle Templar; I'll ride him back up to the house. Several boys wanted to pet the horse, and Lord Henry obliged them. Thomas wanted to sit astride but was discouraged due to his lack of experience.

After a few more minutes, Lord FitzRoy tipped his hat, mounted, and trotted away. Lord FitzRoy made nine new friends that day.

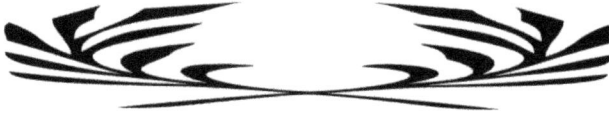

CHAPTER III

GRAFTON FOREST

A week following the visit good weather returned to Grafton Manor. Days were cool, but the abundant sunshine made it pleasant to be outdoors. Horton was repairing tack for the planting season to commence.

Henry strolled into the barn from the north end, nearest the Manor house.

"Mr. Weatherford," he called out loudly.

"Yes, sir, your lordship?" Horton replied.

"Anything on the forest yet," he asked.

"Well," Horton came back, "I have something that keeps coming back to me. To be honest, it seems silly to me."

The two stood side by side. Horton was reluctant to begin.

"Speak up, man! What have you in mind?" Lord FitzRoy prodded.

Hesitantly Horton began, "Well, sir, it came to me, there are no hunting lodges in all of England that I know of that may be rented for short periods. The peerages are at the mercy of invitations from family or acquaintances to have such a place to go. Even fewer have such a place of their own. Might the use of such a place bring in a goodly rental?

A lodge for the fox hunters—with stables for the horses and dogs—they might stay for days. It might be something in which clans, groups, or just men wishing to hunt would have an interest."

He stopped; his face reddened slightly for fear of reproach. Looking at Horton, Lord FitzRoy propped one arm on the other and rested his chin on his fist in imagination.

After about a minute he spoke, "What an odd idea." He paused once more and said, "But, I think you may be on to something. I recall one—Henry the VIII's, ironically, at Bow, Bromley Hall. Yet, that wasn't public. The forest simply has no use that I can see, except exactly that for which it was created." He paused to envision it, speaking aloud, "A gentlemen's lodge." Then he smiled good-naturedly adding, "No offense toward the ladies, but at times they are a pesky lot."

With that, Horton smiled from ear to ear and cleared his throat.

Henry began again, nodding his head in approval, "Thank you, Mr. Weatherford." And with that, Henry turned, going back to the house. In his mind, he was already spinning out pieces of a plan. He was convinced. Putting it to paper was the next step.

Horton, his confidence boosted by the successful presentation of his Grafton Forest plan to Lord Henry, now presumed to propose Jenkins' request about the children. He spoke to Lord FitzRoy about Thomas, Elizabeth, and Laddie coming to the manor. He reiterated the Hamsteads' need for relief and the manor needing more hands in the fields, work appropriate for Thomas and Laddie. Elizabeth at 12 was big for her age and strong and could serve well as a scullery maid.

Three days later Horton received his answer.

"Mr. Weatherford, this is a new idea for us, caring for children this age."

"Thank you, your Lordship," Horton quickly answered. "Tillie and I will keep and tend to them as foster parents."

"Not so fast; we will grant them a 30-day trial period. Having met the children, I feel Thomas is the stronger, but Laddie is the most amicable. Elizabeth is young, but she can have a try. I believe we shan't pay them until we know their worth. You can help with that. Does that seem fair?"

"Sir, that is very gracious. It will help the family tremendously.

To be candid, your lordship, Thomas, is the one eating them out of house and home. I will send word, telling you when I expect them to arrive. I feel it a personal favor to me as well, and I will see they don't abuse your trust," concluded Horton.

"Have them take their meals with the manor staff. That should be helpful for Tillie," Lord FitzRoy offered as he turned to go.

"Yes, sir, your lordship," replied Horton.

Cecilia felt a twinge in her heart when informed that three children were coming to the manor. Being around children near the ages of hers, had they lived, unnerved her considerably.

She protested to Henry, "I don't think I can manage my feelings with such a situation. It makes me feel as though I have betrayed my babies. At our age, I am resigned to our lot. But to have these children will hurt more than I can bear. Please don't have them come."

Even so, Lord Henry had already agreed to the plan with Horton. He explained it to Cecilia as merely a business decision.

A fortnight later Lord FitzRoy instructed Horton to plan a trip to the new land, to study and further consider the idea of a lodge. Henry drew some ideas of what it might look like.

Horton asked of him, "Do we go staying over a night, or return the same day?"

"I hadn't considered it overnight, but I believe I like the idea. Two hundred sixty hectares is a sizable area. We will likely spend a great deal of the day ascertaining the exact location," Henry remarked.

Settling for Thursday the next week, they would travel with a single-horse cart for their goods and two hired hands.

Lady Cecelia was not pleased that Henry would go to the forest but understood the need to survey the area. She was still hurt that Henry had accepted the children. Tillie was unsettled by it, but knew Horton was at Lord FitzRoy's beck and call.

Next Thursday morning before sun-up they set off. After an hour they reached Kingsdown Road and turned right. It was shortly realized that without their surveyor's maps, the trek would have been impossible. Even so, several stops were required to make inquiries to the locals about their destination.

In the late morning they finally found the first peg of a surveyor's marking, the one which signified the southwest corner. It was shaped like parallelogram being somewhat in line with the English Channel. However, none of it reached the seashore. After spending the remaining day roaming the forest, a high point was found from which the North Sea could be seen to the east.

Looking at the surrounding area inspired Lord Henry. He animatedly slapped his thigh and verbalized his lofty vision. "This rocky high spot is just the place to build" he exclaimed. "What say you, Mr. Weatherford?"

"It would depend on the structure built and how it and the grounds were laid out. But, yes, sir, this seems the place. And as well, with an abundance of rock, a roadbed could be laid from Kingsdown Road south to this site.

Lord FitzRoy noted, "Kingsdown Inn would be just one mile north of the lodge – hopefully, a friendly place to put one's feet up and have a beer and fish and chips if you liked. I've asked, and it seems hardly anyone visits Kingsdown due to its seclusion. With the lodge established, business is likely to pick up for them."

"We're beginning to lose the light. We best get settled in, don't you think, sir?" Horton suggested.

Lord FitzRoy wanted to sleep on the wagon. Horton thought it was because of his fear of ground animals in the night. Horton and the field hands each put up a tent and set small logs along its edges.

Soon a fire blazed, pushing back the shadowy figures of the evening until darkness took its full effect. Stars and the full moon lent comfort as they ate bread and cheese with some dried mutton.

Lord Henry and Horton each took two fingers of a fine Jamaican Rum following the meal. They verbally built and rebuilt the lodge, adding and altering its amenities.

"And what shall I call it?" asked Lord FitzRoy.

Names flew for a time. Horton, with the subsequent enthusiastic agreement of the two farmhands, suggested. "Grafton Forest." Its name means 'woodland settlement," Horton boasted.

Quietly they considered it. No objection was heard.

An hour passed, and the conversation labored as one by one, each requested to be excused to retire for the night.

Upon their return home the next day, Henry composed a list of what the lodge might entail. He envisioned it thus:

1. First floor – 800 sq. yds., including wings.

2. Second floor—600sq. yds., including wings.
3. Third floor and widow's watch—100 sq. yds. with considerable glass on the east front, south side, and west front overlooking the North Sea and the Dover Strait.
4. Double fireplace on the first floor large enough to stand two horses side by side and firedogs two yards in length.
5. Exterior of first floor to be stone.
6. Exterior of second and third floors to be logs.
7. Sleeping chambers, 25, no less than 180 sq. ft.
8. Bed chambers for royalty and nobility, no less than 320 sq. ft. each with two suites on the first two floors, each with fireplace.
9. Interior kitchen for winter, exterior kitchen for summer with scullery between.
10. First floor porch along south front elevation.
11. Two water closets on the first and second floors.
12. Stables for 14 horses, including tack room outfitted for storage and repair.
13. Staircase in the center of the first floor three yards wide to the third floor.
14. Exotic taxidermy mounts, including prized game trophies from personal collection, featured around the great hall,

He concluded his thoughts with the assurance that a quarry just two miles away would provide all the cut white stone needed. There was more than enough. Once removed, it would leave a large pool that would become the center of a magnificent garden.

Shortly after the basics were decided, Henry set about to find such a man as could build his lodge and its curtilage. The plans were drawn and delivered to a building firm in London. The firm delivered their proposal to Lord FitzRoy as requested. The firm estimated the cost to be £350,000.

CHAPTER IV

THOMAS AND LADDIE LOOK TO THE FUTURE

Following the last frost of the season construction began in 1852. Henry visited the site at least once a week to view the laborious progress. Lady Cecilia wished to manage the décor appointments which was agreeable with Henry.

The three Hamstead children were moved to the Weatherfords' home. Moving was an unsettling process; however, it offered far more space, a small room for each child. It proved after 30 days to be a good arrangement. Thereafter, the children were paid a penny a week to work the farm with the promise of more as their proficiency improved. As well, it included full board and keep. It wasn't much, but the opportunity to live at Grafton Manor meant much excitement to the three even though they were prohibited entry to the main house except by the request of the FitzRoys.

Little was seen or heard from Lady Cecilia following the arrival of the children. It was not clear what she did with her time, but she certainly wasn't in the company of the children. They were never mentioned in her presence.

Elizabeth wasn't well-suited for fieldwork. She was frequently accused by the boys of not pulling her weight and endured their rude remarks. She was transferred to a scullery maid position. Though young, she did a fine job in the main house.

On an afternoon in June, Elizabeth was replacing cookware when Thomas snuck in the scullery door, taking a seat where he wasn't likely to be seen. He had a developing fondness for Elizabeth.

Elizabeth espied him but did nothing to acknowledge him outright; she secretly smiled at the attention. She continued storing away the cookware. Elizabeth stepped to the footstool near Thomas, and stretched up, to place a crock on the top shelf.

Thomas eyeballed her leg nearly to the knee, and without even a whisper of a thought, slid his left hand up the backside of her leg to the crease of her buttock, smiling like a possum eating persimmons.

Elizabeth screamed as though bitten by a viper, bringing her left hand down with the crock which struck Thomas' forehead just above the left eye.

He fell backward, unconscious, to the floor as blood spurted from the gash. The crock broke as well.

Elizabeth came down from the footstool loudly crying out, "Madelina—Madelina! Come quick! I've killed Thomas.

It was an accident." She dropped to the floor to see if he were dead.

"He *is* breathing," she cried.

Madelina knelt to examine his head and stem the flow of blood with a cloth.

"What happened?" she asked as she turned her attention to Elizabeth. Two kitchen maids looked on; one had observed it all and the other, upon hearing the clatter, had looked up to see Thomas on the floor. They all waited to see what Missus Wallander, who had just entered the room, would do. She was calm but irritated as she examined Thomas.

Elizabeth, in tears, began, "I was placing the pot on the shelf when it fell."

She hadn't yet decided to tell what Tom had done.

"You shouldn't stretch, placing pots up there. Ask someone to help. And you should have used a ladder," she admonished. "Place a cold compress on his face. I expect he will regain consciousness soon." Elizabeth genuflected to her.

The two maids whispered to one another and then were quiet.

Caroline, the maid who had seen it all, could contain herself no longer and charged Elizabeth, "Tell Missus Wallander the whole story, Elizabeth. He can't be allowed to do that sort of thing."

Missus Wallander's face drew cold as stone awaiting someone to speak.

Timidly, Elizabeth drew a deep breath and reached for the courage to tell. She liked Tom and didn't want to cause him any trouble.

"Ma'am, Tom surprised me. He ran his hand under my skirt, up my leg," she recounted shyly. "I wasn't harmed, but it surprised me."

Missus Wallander, crimson with anger, spoke harshly to Tom, who was regaining consciousness. "Thomas, what were you doing in the house? Leave now and tell Horton what you have done. Tell him I require an adequate punishment for your behavior. My suggestion would be a horsewhipping."

Thomas tried but couldn't rise. The two girls helped him to his feet as he staggered from the room, cloth still pressed tightly to his head.

Thomas foolishly waited. Maybe good fortune would intervene on his behalf; maybe the world would end. Horton didn't know of the incident until late that evening.

As darkness began to fall, Thomas approached Horton at work in the barn brushing out the Lipizzaner. "Mr. Horton?" Thomas mumbled, "Missus Wallander sent me. I have to tell you why."

"What is it, Thomas?" he asked with piqued curiosity.

Thomas hesitantly began and, as smoothly and quickly as he could, laid out the basics of the matter in the simplest words possible and painted a picture of innocent fun.

Horton reflected for a moment. With his back to Thomas, he smiled as he remembered the times he'd wanted to do such a thing, but never had. Horton composed himself and turned toward Thomas.

"Do you understand how terrible such an act is?"

"Yes, Sir, I do now," Thomas replied.

"So, I'm to punish you? Help me with a way to impress upon you the importance of common civility and proper conduct toward ladies," Horton prompted.

"She said you should horsewhip me, but that's extreme. Isn't it?" he added hopefully.

"I think so. Most important is your coming to terms with respectful behavior toward women.

I have an idea; what about a sincere apology to Elizabeth in the presence of Missus Wallander? And a penance forfeiting four weeks of your stipend. Could we do that?" Horton asked.

Thomas squirmed and momentarily fidgeted about before responding in a subdued tone, "Yes."

"Then I think we're good to go. Okay?" Horton searched Thomas' face for agreement.

"Yes, sir," responded Thomas. He slothfully returned to the house.

Later that evening Tillie and Horton enjoyed a good laugh. It had gone well.

On an early March morn' the staff was seated in the servants' hall at 6:00 as breakfast was about to be taken. Circulating was a week-old copy of the *Daily Telegraph*, a London newspaper.

A headline jumped out, catching Laddie's eye. He read it twice to be sure he understood. The notice advised that cabin boys and the like were needed by the navy. Interested parties should apply at the dockyard of the Royal Naval College, in Portsmouth. He had dozed off many a night with just this idyllic dream.

"Thomas, look at this!" directed Laddie, "What do you think? Should we leave and go seek our fortunes at sea?"

HMS Hood was seeking boys Thomas and Laddie's age to work as cabin boys, swabbies, powder monkeys, errand boys, and in general work in spaces too small for full-sized men.

Thomas looked at it, but his affect showed no interest. "I confess I'd like to leave here, but I want to be something better than a sea dog. Besides, Elizabeth and I are talking of marriage in a year or so," Thomas replied.

"Aw, go on, you two aren't old enough to marry," Laddie chided. "You're not yet 17, and she just turned 13. What do you know of marriage?"

"I know what I need to know," he spat back with a twinkle in his eyes and a small smile in the corner of his mouth."

"Okay," shouted Madelina, "Clear the room and get about your duties."

Quickly the boys headed off to see if they could get a front seat on one of the two wagons that were headed to the bean fields. Horton climbed to the front seat of the first wagon, reins in hand.

They needed to be in the fields by seven. The fields were already buzzing with activity. Horton's crew numbered 25, including Laddie and Thomas.

Laddie fixated on how he was going to get aboard the *HMS Hood*, daydreaming about famous men who had joined up that way. He learned that the navy was based southwest of London in Portsmouth.

The next day after his field work, he posted a request for information. As the courier went his way, Laddie felt little confidence. He was impatient and wondered which would come first—a response to his letter or the rapture of the saints.

For no good reason Laddie and Thomas' relationship became strained. Their divergent interests and perception of each other's statuses created the friction. Though Laddie held no interest in Elizabeth and wasn't intruding, Thomas resented Laddie's haughty attitude about his naval prospects. Thomas, the senior of the two, strutted before Elizbeth at every opportunity.

One Monday morning it came to a head. Laddie was about to board the first wagon. As he reached up to grasp the back of the seat to mount the wagon, something got hold of the waistband of his breeches, yanking him back to the ground. Thomas proceeded to mount the wagon in his place.

But as a leopard attacks its prey, Laddie pounced on him, and they both fell back to the ground, pounding and scuffling. Horton only saw Laddie pounce on Thomas and sent Laddie to the back of the second wagon. The dust settled, and they commenced their trip to the field.

The lodge would be completed by the end of March. It was rumored that guests were coming to Grafton Forest in late May. The staff was given a heads-up as the lodge needed to be put in order. It would double the ordinary household workload.

Only the family, Maximillian, and Missus Wallander knew the identity of the party which would include a head of state and his family as the first guests. James Parke was the First Baron of Wensleydale. He began his life peerage as Baron in 1850. After an education at The King's School, Macclesfield, Trinity College, and Cambridge, he studied under a special pleader before being called to the Bar by the Inner Temple in 1813. He was appointed to the Court of King's Bench on 28 November 1828; he became a Privy Counsellor in 1833. One year later, he rose to a Baron of the Treasury. He was a lifelong friend to Lord FitzRoy.

To entertain Baron Parke and his family would give Grafton Forest a good start with the promise of many illustrious guests to follow.

Finishing touches such as extravagant landscaping, stone walkways to the garden, riding paths, and special treatment to the widow's watch were ten days to two weeks away. Grafton Forest progressed well and would impress.

Interior appointments were delayed. For Cecilia many hard decisions lingered. She was bringing a lady's touch, and

Henry thought it too fastidious and too costly. He gave way to her far more than he liked. He hoped, after a time, to make some alterations. Admittedly Lady Cecilia had done wonders with the grounds. She hired Millie Corbet, a master gardener, to help lay out an exquisite theme.

Cecilia and Henry received word the Baron would spend one week, arriving from London on a Sunday, the 24th of May. Baron's family extended their stay to two weeks at the invitation of Lord Henry. It turned into an enormously large family holiday.

Grafton Forest earned the praises of Baron Parke and consequently an excellent reputation to their mutual friends and acquaintances in London.

The week following the Baron's letter, Laddie received his response from the Royal Navy. The prerequisites were: some primary school, aged between 10 and 16, weighing 7 stone or more, obligated for two years, and no criminal history. It was favorable. Laddie should report on 6 January, 1854. He was told to assemble at building number 309, Portsmouth Pier.

On his person he must provide three letters of recommendation—one from a vestryman, one from the local sheriff, indicating that he wasn't a vagabond, and finally, a letter from his guardian verifying his date of birth at less than 17 years. These seemingly insurmountable tasks threw him into a panic. Horton assured him there would be no problem.

The jealousy of Thomas flared with the receipt of Laddie's navy letter. It exacerbated unnecessary hostility. Horton managed the conflict between the two the best he could. He praised Laddie's courage moving ahead with his navy plan.

CHAPTER V

THE WAR AND PROMOTIONS

Lord FitzRoy, hearing of Laddie's ambitions, took him aside one day.

"So your plan is to join Her Majesty's Navy." Lord FitzRoy's forthcoming manner overwhelmed Laddie, and he could only nod in agreement.

"There is no greater opportunity than to join in the defense of our Queen and Country. Many prodigious men have advanced in peerage and favor through military service. Approach it as a life's goal and not a job, and you will go far. I like your grit," Lord FitzRoy enthused. He asked, "Laddie, how will you go about it?"

Emboldended by Lord FitzRoy's grand declaration Laddie spoke, "Lord FitzRoy, pardon my boast, sir, but I know I'm made of finer stuff. I know not the risk I'll encounter, but, your lordship, I want to make my parents and all of you proud. I'm moving into a man's world, and I'd ask if you all would call me 'Laird' instead of Laddie. I'd be obliged to you if you could do that for me."

"Yes, oh yes, I'd be pleased to," Lord FitzRoy agreed with knowing amusement. Lord FitzRoy gazed at Laddie with a silent reminiscence of his own youth then remarked, "God be with you, Laddie. Sorry, I mean Laird."

Laddie's manner brought a nostalgic sentiment that lingered with Lord FitzRoy and a curiosity about the boy's heritage. He might inquire with Horton about "Laird's" history.

Thomas treated Laddie with indignation. He taunted Laddie with remarks like, "While you're sleeping in the smelly hold of a ship, I'll be sleeping with Elizabeth." It stung, but Laddie sensed there would be a tomorrow, and he would be at the better end of it.

Lord FitzRoy placed his first advertisement for the lodge in the *Daily Telegraph*. The notice was substantial and certain to garner attention. It spoke of the enchanting forest with trees as old as England herself and a view of the Dover Strait at the North Sea. Hunting and fishing abound. The beautiful garden and grounds include stables for 14 horses with tack room. Interior amenities include 25 sleeping rooms, four suites, massive fireplaces, two kitchens, and water closets. Guides could be hired for the adventurous. Inquiries should be addressed to the land agent with prompt replies to be forthcoming.

Lord FitzRoy employed a married couple without children to reside at the lodge. They were from Canterbury, William, and Lidia Wellington.

William was well suited for such duty, being retired from a rifle regiment of Her Majesty's Army. They tended to the basic needs of the property. Any problems went first to them to resolve and on to Lord FitzRoy should help be needed. It further provided security for the grounds.

By the end of June the land agent had received a dozen inquiries which was encouraging.

The acquisition of the three letters Laddie needed took longer than he expected, but it was accomplished. Horton was proud of Laddie and treated him well during the time remaining with them. With Horton's help, Laddie secured passage to Portsmouth from Dover. A passing coal barge was to arrive January 2nd, four days before he reported at Portsmouth. His obligation for passage was to assist the crew of the freighter with errands and small jobs ordered by the first mate, a fine arrangement.

Lord FitzRoy's 60th birthday celebration was postponed due to the crush of interest and activity at the lodge. Sixty was so difficult to accept and seemed a turning point for him. A dinner in his honor was set for late October.

By November there were two guests at the lodge each month. Few stayed more than a week. Even for the well-to-do the rate of £100 a night or the weekly rate of £600 stung a bit. The lodge was furnished, but no other amenities were provided. A stay at the lodge generally necessitated guests to bring a full complement of household staff from the butler and housekeeper to the footmen, maids, and cook.

Between guests Lady Cecilia sent her own house maids to clean and refurbish the lodge. It was profitable. Henry and Cecilia frequented the lodge themselves, staying one or two days at a time. Their favorite room, the widow's watch opened onto an ocean breeze. They enjoyed the view of ships navigating up and down the channel.

Elizabeth moved up to assistant cook, working with Mrs. Burton, and received a small increase in wages. Thomas continued to be more than adequate help for Horton, shadowing his every activity.

Laird had been away with the Navy for several months to complete his training. His first real adventure began in March, the Crimean War.

The belligerents were Russia against France, England, Turkey, and Piedmont-Sardinia. The Crimean War reshaped Europe's power structure. Russian pressure on Turkey in turn threatened British commercial and strategic interests in the Middle East.

The outbreak of violence arose from various factors including the issue of Christian minority rights in the Holy Land, the overall declining Ottoman Empire leading to the "eastern question," and resistance of the British and French to Russian expansion.

Generally, this meant little to Laird. He was enlisted, excelled in his classes, and one month ago was promoted to Boy 2 with a small increase in his monthly stipend.

The thought of war brought several feelings over the young sailors. In the childlike portion of their minds, it gave them a feeling of the romance of conflict and the first draw of blood. Eventually, it subsided to concern and then to fear. They couldn't speak of the fear, however. The very word did not exist in their vocabulary. Yet it began to rule over them night and day in the horror of dreams and during daily chores.

So many bodies dismembered, but certainly not their own. Over time the horrors came alive, casting vivid images in their imaginations. Could these be their own bodies lying cold, with parts and pieces scattered here and there? And among the remnants, portions of their heads with sightless eyes?

Horton received an unexpected but extremely welcome letter from Laddie.

14 August 1854

Horton,

It's much different than I thought. I expected it to be exciting, and it is, but I didn't think people would be so rough. Most of them I wouldn't want to meet at night on a side street in London. I won't say they scare me, but they do keep me on the lookout both day and night.

There are three of us sea boys or, as you and I said, cabin boys. Manny is 14 and just a wee bit smaller than me. He's ranked a 3. I'm ranked a 2. The oldest is Burton, and he's ranked 1. We get promoted if we do well. The additional few coins is nothing to get excited about.

Like we talked, we boys do all the dirty work like cleaning the head, mopping vomit, and kitchen help when they say.

There's a man we think is a bloody invert. He's taken a liking to Manny. Manny's on to him and avoids him. I don't know if my letters are read by anyone else so, I shan't say more about that here.

When I signed up, I changed my name to Laird. Laddie doesn't suit me here. I know it's a stretch, but I like it. So, write me at HMS *Beagle*, Portsmouth, Laird Hamstead, Boy 2. I'm sure you realize we rarely get or send mail unless we cross paths with a ship going north to Portsmouth. It happens maybe twice a month.

I would like to know if Thomas is making headway with Elizabeth. I like her, but if she sees something in the likes of him, then she's not the one for me. You can tell him I think he's a bugger if he can't leave her alone.

Burton just told me we're coming upon a sloop northbound. I must stop if I want this to go today. We're headed to Istanbul, I think.

I've got so many questions but no time. Tell all hello from me and that I'm doing well so far.

Take care of yourself,

Laird

The HMS *Beagle*, a 10-gun brig sloop, was launched in May 1820. She was of the barque class rigging with three main masts. She was 27.5 yards long and 7.5 yards at the beam, draughting 3.8 yards empty. At top speed, she could make six to seven knots under normal conditions.

The ship was used in the coronation of King George IV as she passed under London Bridge. Her first Captain was Flag Lieutenant Robert FitzRoy, a 23-year-old aristocrat who proved to be an able commander.

Laird and his mates had explored her stem to stern, and by the time they were out one month, they were very familiar with every square inch of the vessel. It was a pleasure to see each compartment, but moreso, they must be acquainted with all of her. Often, they were called upon to fetch or simply carry equipment or orders to the crew or officers.

They were three days out before they lost sight of the English coastline, all in perfect weather. As they turned south in the Celtic Sea, the weather turned on them. Storms overtook them with torrential rains from the west, pushing them toward France.

During the greatest of tempests, the helmsman was the only man on deck and at the wheel much of the time. At its worst he would tie her off, after which he descended, closing the hatch, with monumental waves breaking over the bow, spraying her from stem to stern.

Tension was present throughout the ship, and the three young sailors would remain in their small room, waiting out the tumultuous conditions. Hardly anyone ventured from the mid-cabin unless called on.

Few storms lasted more than one or two hours, and then all hands were called on deck to repair or clean the mess that remained from loose ropes and rigging.

After being storm-battered, it was odd to break out into the bright sunlight with seas as smooth as glass. It seemed like a whole new day. It would brighten all spirits.

Next, the navigator brought out the sextant to find their position. During daylight no landmarks were available, but the position of the sun and the sundial helped. At night it was rather easy to find their location with stars and the moon.

That evening they found they'd strayed easterly, off course nearly five nautical miles, not a problem for them.

Over the next week they made good time and were on course for the inlet of the Mediterranean. Off the port lay the coast of Spain at longitude north 43.353 and latitude west 9.876.

Having survived the storm, the young sailors were lax and began behaving childishly. Burton carelessly left open a small drain door in the head. Water flowed backward in from the sea. Perhaps 2,000 liters flowed into the forward hull.

The seawater wasn't visible for it lay under the flooring. Four hands were dispatched and entered the head. Submerged, one man closed the shut-off due to the eventual risk of scuttling the ship. With buckets, the head was emptied and lastly mopped dry by the three young sailors.

No serious harm was done. But had it not been timely discovered, it could have sunk the ship. Not a man was surprised when Burton, Boy 1, was summoned aft to the captain's quarters. In the captain's quarters, Burton stood like a beam of wood without movement looking straight ahead. He saluted and offered, "Sir."

The deathly quiet terrorized Burton.

"Youth is no excuse for your action. You're to be keelhauled for thirty minutes at sun-up. As well, your rank is reduced to Boy 3. You're excused. First mate, take him to the brig and secure him for the morning," Then fetch me Hamstead." The first mate grasped Burton's arm, practically dragging him from the room.

Fifteen minutes later, came a timid knock at the cabin door.

"Enter," called the captain.

The door opened and in stepped Laird, coming to attention with a salute and, "Sir."

"Let this be a lesson to you. On the sea, there is no child's play. I am promoting you to Boy 1. You will see to my needs. If I summon you, I will expect you at my door within two minutes.

Clean yourself up. You look terrible. Report here at half-past seven in the morning. Are we clear?" bellowed the captain at Laird.

"Yes, sir," responded Laird trembling slightly.

"You're excused," loudly replied the captain.

Laird saluted, did a round-about, and left, his mind about to explode with feelings of joy and terror and pity for Burton.

CHAPTER VI

CAPTAIN FITZROY AND LAIRD HAMSTEAD

The next morning Laird was awake early. He had washed his uniform and hat the evening before. With the uniform dry and stretched, he dressed and did all he could to look his best, all before seven.

When he thought it was half-past seven, he knocked on the captain's door to hear the command, "Enter."

He did, and standing, he saluted, saying, "Sir?"

"Find the first mate and have him assemble the men at the stern with the prisoner." With that, the captain put on his jacket and left the room.

The captain took his place at the center of the stern. Laird stood back two paces and to his left. Burton was stripped to his waist and held fast with two ropes, one tied to each wrist. The captain, in view of the first mate, nodded

Four men picked up Burton by his limbs, carried him to the edge of the stern, and on the count of three heaved him away to the water four yards below.

Following the rough toss, the sound of his body splashing upon the water was drowned by the wake of the ship. He had landed on his back, struggling to keep his head up to breathe.

The clock began 30 minutes.

Except for a northbound ship and transfer of mail, the rest of the day was quiet.

Burton remained in his quarters, trying to come to terms with what had fallen out to him and how his career was likely ended.

They followed the coastline of Spain for three days. On the fourth, they turned easterly into the Strait of Gibraltar. In the early afternoon off the port bow of the *Beagle*, and perhaps 20 nautical miles yet to the north, a peak stood alone out of the Mediterranean Sea. On the main deck Laird learned from another mate that the immovable protrusion was the Rock of Gibraltar and the outlining shore was Spain.

Well into the Mediterranean Sea they continued easterly on to their destination, Istanbul. By this time, he had learned their cargo was munitions—enough to convert their vessel to several million toothpicks. That explained the extra care that had been so obvious.

For the next two weeks, they maintained a heading of 86° until they passed Palermo on the starboard side. Several days later, they passed through the Strait of Messina.

The final leg of their journey turned northward across the Aegean Sea, well within the interior of the war.

With cannons readied, crews well-rehearsed, and lookouts posted in the crow's nest, theirs was not to engage anyone but to sneak in under cover of the morning mist, be unloaded, and straight-way return to England, not firing a shot.

Five weeks following Laird's post from the *Beagle*, Horton received the letter. He read it aloud in the servant's hall, excluding the sensitive material.

"Would anyone like to send a note back to Laddie? I will be writing one, and I'm sure he would enjoy hearing from us, especially Elizabeth." He smiled and continued. "He says he has changed his name to Laird. I can understand in the manly company of shipmates, Laddie wouldn't do." A response was posted that included five pages, some not so legible.

As the letters from Horton and the children traveled, the *Beagle* approached Istanbul.

In the first week of November 1854 they were traversing the Sea of Marmara.

Every vessel was under suspicion and avoided. Their docking port was the west bank of Kumkapi. They weighed anchor about three nautical miles from the dock, awaiting a small sloop with a double sail that would come to them and lead them to the proper dock.

Working alongside Captain FitzRoy was exhilarating for Laird. He was privy to most of the ship's information. He thought it the best of all navy schooling.'

The two enjoyed respect for one another, considering age and experience differences. It became common for the captain to have Hamstead nearby. Laird was always ready with a snappy salute. His at-attention appearance presented always its best.

Having dropped anchor before reaching the channel into the Black Sea in Istanbul, little activity occurred in the tense interim.

Laird remained near the captain's door. At the aft window, the captain, telescope in hand, studied a craft to the north. Laird ventured to speak, "Captain, may I have a word,"

The captain turned from the window in response, "Yes, Hamstead?"

Laird asked, "Sir, I wish to continue with Her Majesty's Navy. What must I do to attain to the Navy College at Portsmouth?"

The captain seemed pleased and responded, "See the first mate. He will provide the information you will need." He returned to the aft window.

"Thank you, sir," Laird replied.

Watches had begun days before, one man in the crow's nest exchanging places with the next each six hours beginning from dawn. They spied little, save the occasional British vessel in passing.

Numerous distant battles continued as belligerents sought out one another, fighting to the death. At night the sky lit up 20 to 30 miles to the north as though thunderstorms raged. All knew it was another vessel bound for the bottom. Laird saw the maps, and it seemed to be like a large fishbowl in the middle of the continent.

Finally on Tuesday evening at dusk the watchman on duty called from the above the approach of a sloop; surely this was their contact.

Once tied off, the sloop's captain came aboard and was escorted to FitzRoy's quarters. Laird was present as the captains took their seats. He poured drinks for the two at FitzRoy's direction.

The visiting officer was an old salt, swarthy and wrinkled. He was a Turk with five or six decades as a seaman behind him. His eyes twinkled with sincere appreciation for the gift from England. He began to explain the plan. "At 400 hours, begin your approach. It will be dark enough, and the fog will hide you as you make your way to dock.

We will fly a large red flag to mark your berth. We expect to have you unloaded within 45 minutes. You can be on your way after the last Russian patrol passes. They come through every four to five hours. We wish you the best in leaving between those patrols." He paused, expecting questions.

Captain FitzRoy replied, "I see no problem. We will do the best we can to escape unseen. Thank you, and we wish you the best in your endeavors."

Together, they exited the room walking to the sloop and saluted one another as the Turk disembarked.

Throughout the night every man was on high alert. Long before the appointed time, they were ready, even leaving a few minutes early.

There wasn't a sound from the *Beagle* as they drifted to the dock. Not even one board of the deck creaked.

Laird, first to see the red banner, pointed it out to the captain. Quietly they drifted in and were tied off.

From a nearby building emerged about 50 men who went straightaway to the ship's hold, returning with unmarked boxes of munitions. As the last boxes left the ship, the men disappeared once more into the building.

Ropes were cast off, and the *Beagle* began slowly to move from her berth.

Back out in the Marmara, the sun began its soft glow through the eastern horizon.

A cry broke the silence from the crow's nest, "Vessel to the west, a vessel to the west."

All eyes turned to see an approaching ship coming directly toward them. First mate Warrant Gabbard called out, "It's Russian." The captain commanded, "Every man to battle stations. Ready your cannons. Powder monkeys begin moving in your powder. On my order, we will commence firing at 700 yards unless fired upon first."

All the crew who could, sought places of safety as the cannons were readied.

Nearing 700 yards, the captain ordered, "Fire."

Surprisingly, four of five shells struck the oncoming vessel with varying severity.

"Reload and give her five more," bellowed the captain and echoed the first mate.

An explosion erupted from the magazine of the Russian vessel, and within ten minutes of the early morning haze, nothing was left on the horizon but men hanging to bits and pieces of ship.

Shortly thereafter came the call, "Cease firing."

In haste, the *Beagle* retraced her pathway back to England, not a man was injured. All returned home safely.

At Grafton Manor Lord FitzRoy asked that his curricle be brought to the main house at eight o'clock. He was going to Canterbury to speak with the Hamsteads. His return was planned by way of Kingsdown to see the accommodations and obtain any news relative to the lodge.

Henry asked Cecilia, "Would you like to go to Canterbury with me? I want to visit the Hamsteads. I shan't be very long. Upon my return I'll pass through Kingsdown for a brief stop. I'm curious what the locals think of the lodge. We can check in on the lodge and the Wellingtons on our way home."

"Oh, that sounds so nice, but I can't," she replied. "Lady Thurstan is bringing her eldest niece who will be presented at court next season."

"Ahh," he acknowledged. "I expect to be home by dusk then." He climbed aboard and clucked to the horses. They began to take the slack from the traces, and away went the curricle.

At 9:30 he arrived at the Hamstead's. The home was modest with a high-pitched thatched roof. Truly it was small, but neat and clean.

Some 200 yards behind the house sat the blacksmith's shop. It fronted on the adjacent street. Hearing the ring of a hammer from the shop, Henry strolled to the front of the house poised to knock. Mrs. Hamstead appeared.

"Lord FitzRoy," she exclaimed. "It's a pleasure to see you. I'll fetch Jenkins and be right back."

In a minute, the hammer stopped its ringing, and after three minutes, he stood with her at the door.

"Lord FitzRoy, won't you please come in?" he gestured as he pulled the door open wide.

"Yes, thank you," replied Lord Henry.

He stepped in and was promptly asked to have a seat at the table.

Jenkins spoke, "I was about to come to the house and have tea. Won't you join us?"

"Yes, thank you," Henry responded and to Mrs. Hamstead added, "with a spoon of sugar."

"Will honey do?" she offered.

"Yes," he replied.

"We are so pleased to see you. Have the children been doing well?" Jenkins asked. "News of the children is always welcome," he prompted.

"Yes, they are well and are a blessing for us. They all have achieved better positions and are doing fine, Henry confirmed. "Laddie wouldn't be satisfied until he was released to join Her Majesty's Navy."

"We have had three letters from him. At the first, he joined at the grade of Boy 3. The young ones increase in rank with more experience," Jenkins remarked. "He was promoted to Boy 2, last we heard. It seems odd to us, but he is having the time of his life," continued Jenkins. "He spoke of a trip of at least a year. We pray for him because he may be headed for the Crimean War, you know. It's a nasty business, but the Russians started it, pushin' their way into the Ottoman lands as they did."

"It's Laddie I have come to inquire about," Lord Henry explained. I wondered if he might be related to friends of ours. I'm hopeful you might help me with information about his family."

"Certainly," Mary replied. "However, that was 11 years ago, and he was only four."

"His mother was Aggie McCallister," Jenkins offered.

"Yes," Mary agreed.

"Perchance, was Bancroft her married name?" Henry asked.

"So far as we know, she never married. Not to be unkind to the dead, but she worked at pubs and did other things to provide."

"Were you acquainted with any of her lovers?"

"None as I recall," Mary responded

"Do you know any of her blood family?"

Jenkins answered this time. "I met her brother. Her family had disowned her, and he was trying to help. He wanted to take her home to Birmingham, but she refused, saying the family didn't want her around for the sake of the children."

"She had several friends in Kensington on Market Court. Perhaps someone there might know better than we," Mary added. "We knew her only somewhat the two months before she died. She had no visitors and was often too ill to be understood in her speech.

We called him Laddie because he was a wee little fellow to start and gave him our last name to help him. She told us he had been christened Robert Raphaël.

She was gone before we knew it. Forty-two I think she was. We don't know his father's name. She didn't want to shame him, him being from a proud family and all. She never said. She insisted that he had promised to provide for her, but he didn't—not that we know of."

The conversation waned until Jenkins brought up a question.

"Lord FitzRoy, we have a question for you. Seeing as how well things went with three of our older children, we have a boy, 16, whom we believe will be another good farmhand."

Mary carefully entreated him, "Are you in a position to have another youngster at the manor?"

"May I meet him?" he asked.

"He's at school and won't return home this evening until late," she replied.

"Have him speak to Horton. If Horton looks on it favorably, I will certainly grant your request," Lord FitzRoy assured.

Shortly thereafter Lord FitzRoy excused himself, explaining that he needed to go to Kingsdown.

"I would like to know what manner of business they have. Do you know of it?" he asked.

"They've no blacksmith but one mercantile store and a small market in season. It's a quiet and simple place with nice folks," Jenkins volunteered. "Mostly I see them when they bring their smithy trade to me."

CHAPTER VII

LORD HENRY STILL ANXIOUS FOR AN HEIR

Henry wasn't surprised as he entered Kingsdown noting a shabby tavern, the mercantile Jenkins had referenced, and a rather rickety dock. Thereon a man sat on a barrel mending a net, a man whom Henry thought might be the dock owner. He rode up to him and greeted him with a, "Good afternoon, friend."

The stranger nodded and continued weaving.

"I can see a little more trade wouldn't hurt Kingsdown. I'm your neighbor. My people built the lodge south of here," Henry told him.

The old man stopped and laid down his work.

"I hope that means we will see more business. We're all just hanging on. There are 16 families around town. Most are fishermen. We do have a fine dairy east of here that employs several," the old man added.

"We don't have regular employees so much, but when visitors come to the lodge, we need several to keep things on the move," Henry offered, "I'd like to show it to you sometime."

"I suspect, out here in the hinterland, you'll not find many who'll be wanting a room," he told Henry.

Henry said nothing but realized his neighbor had no idea what was about to happen.

"I've not introduced myself. I'm Lord Henry FitzRoy. My home is the Grafton Manor, about eight miles west of Kingsdown. We farm mostly."

"Well, it's a pleasure to meet you and to see more folk coming to our little part of the Kingdom. I'm Merwin McKenzie. We came here from Scotland in '97. The clan bickering was too much for the family," Merwin shared. "Yes, I'd be pleased to see your cabin when next I'm down that way."

Henry looked to see the sun only slightly over the tree line.

"I'd best be on my way home. Being my first time here, I don't have a feel for how long I'll be. My wife, Cecilia, will be expecting me by dark. I've enjoyed myself and making your acquaintance."

"The same with me also. Have a good evening," Merwin replied, and the curricle was off at a trot.

Cecilia and Henry were going to London the first week of November. Henry had information on the farm operation for the agriculture secretary. As well, he wanted to visit Peter.

The farm took on two more hands. One was the older child, Evan, whom the Hamsteads had suggested. It wasn't likely he would be with them long, however. He was bright, a scholar, and handsome. No doubt he was destined for a high-ranking job far above farming.

Elizabeth noticed him soon enough and smiled each time she looked his way.

Thomas noticed and felt uneasy about him. It was evident after a week that Thomas wasn't as cocky as he had been. Evan was nearly a year younger than Thomas but several pounds heavier.

Tillie and Horton were well but still had no children of their own. Tending for the young farmhands and Elizabeth provided them a family of their own. Occasionally Thomas acted out but was more talk than anything. He dared not butt heads with Horton. Horton, a large man anyway, could rip Thomas from end to end, and Thomas knew it full well.

Away in London once more, Cecilia visited old friends; she was a guest at two homes. It seemed every afternoon someone held a tea to attend. She spent more days in London due to the general disagreement between her and Lord Henry over having children on the farm.

Countess Dedra Smothers asked Cecilia, "I've heard of your lodge. It sounds like a very rough place to visit. Is it as coarse as it sounds?"

"Well, yes, it is in some ways. Yet all the modern facilities are available. I like to sum it up this way. If you enjoy going back in time, the sound of birds in the trees, a perpetual breeze from the coast all day long, and peaceful scenery, then it's the place. When we take a notion, which isn't often, we go up for a night or two. The North Sea and Strait of Dover are most glorious from the widow's watch.

If you would like to visit, I'd be happy to entertain you there for a day or two. It's a place for groups of up to 60," Cecilia told her. "Or if only a couple wished to visit, that would be agreeable as well."

Dedra was interested. Cecilia could read it in her face.

"It sounds wonderful. I will speak to Reginald about it. Perhaps after a review we could take our family for a visit," Dedra replied.

"Oh, I neglected to mention we have stables for horses. It's complete with a full tack room and supplies."

In the weeks that followed, a rumor circulated that Cecilia and Lord Henry were estranged. No one knew why, not even the house staff. Some thought Cecilia wished to adopt a child. Indeed, she wanted a child and was continually depressed by it; they had no hopes of one. Henry expressed concern enough but felt that in time a solution would arrive.

Lady Cecilia busied herself with charitable work in London. She became a nursing assistant in a facility treating the injured returning from the war. She asked Katherine to accompany her by train from Dover. She began staying the week, returning home on Saturdays. Her driver, Edger, picked them up at Dover upon her return.

Lady Cecilia was an excellent help and encouraged the men. She tended to Major Casteel attentively, an officer of the artillery. They were good counsel for one another. They shared the loss of children and encouraged faithfulness till God should lift that darkness from them.

One Saturday evening as Henry and Cecilia reclined in the drawing-room, Henry turned to Cecilia, saying, "You know the redheaded child called Laddie? Laddie's red hair is as mine was at one time. My brothers were gingers as well. It may be mad, but I have a feeling of kinship with him. I know how that must sound, but I do."

"What do you find in common other than hair color?" she inquired.

"Familiarity. It seems odd, but I can't let it go."

"I see," she replied in a contemplative tone.

"When first he arrived, I had the strangest feeling I knew him from somewhere, however impossible that must be. He reminds me of my second cousin Robert at that age. I've considered how our minds trick us, but I would like to explore his lineage. I feel strongly about it. What do you think of that?"

She was silent, thinking, wondering where it might lead.

"And you believe he may be related by some means to you?" she inquired.

"He is the spitting image of Robert FitzRoy's much younger brother at that age. Would you think it unwise to look into it?"

Once more, she considered Henry's remarks.

"I cannot speak for how you feel," she stated, "but it seems a harmless pursuit. If nothing is gained, then the cost is little. With the matter resolved we are none the worse."

"I will ask Peter to inquire about this. He has resources to investigate such matters. I would like to make the attempt. You know I value your thoughts."

"Not at all; stranger things have come to fruition— particularly our meeting as it was," she added and smiled at him.

That settled it. When next he should be with Peter in London, he would engage him to investigate.

One by one the lights of the house flickered as the pair made their way to the bedchamber, climbing in, and pulling the curtains around them for warmth. The household staff continued to snuff lamps and candles and secure the manor, making their way to each's respective quarters.

Three weeks later Lord Henry and Peter met. In a private room at the Boar's Head Tavern in London, they convened over fish and chips. Following a greeting and a mug of beer, Peter asked, "So, you're interested in finding someone?"

"Yes," answered Henry.

Peter opened his case, removing a paper for notes.

"I am prompted to do this because I 'm in need of an heir, as you know. I need to find a blood relative, preferably a FitzRoy."

Lord Henry began to recite family lineage going back decades. He presented several parchments of genealogy for the most recent 100 years. He explained the arrival of a boy who reminded him of family, prompting him to be more aggressive in his search.

Following Henry's presentation, Peter commenced with questions. The two continued for two more hours. Lord Henry left out nothing of his family, the good or the bad, as well as the little he knew about the boy. Peter felt intimidated by the daunting task and the likelihood nothing would turn up.

"I must ask for a retainer of £500. There will be expenses such as staff to process the results of each road we go down."

Lord Henry was visibly taken aback. Recovering, he replied, "Well, if we must, we must. If we fail, we fail. However, if we succeed, the cost will be a pittance for the good it will bring."

Peter quickly drafted in his own hand an agreement for the engagement.

"Please sign this contract, and we'll be on our way. You may send payment by courier in a few days," Peter offered.

Upon their parting, Peter put a good face on it and promised, "I will get right to it."

The men shook hands as they left the pub, going their ways.

Each passing year had brought greater concern regarding an heir. He should have done this much earlier.

In London, Peter sought families with the last name McCallister.

He had already traveled to visit the Hamsteads who could add little to what he knew. But one oddity stood out; Laddie would sometimes brag to them that his mother was famous though no one paid it any mind.

Peter had used that visit as an opportunity to stay the night at Grafton Forest. He confessed to Lord Henry later he had never been in a more beautiful and enchanting setting in the fall. He hoped to return with his extended family for several days.

Two weeks passed when on a Saturday evening Peter sat alone at a small table near the window in the Boar's Head with fish and chips. The room was filled with boisterous patrons practically shouting to one another and barmaids moving about at almost a run.

By chance at a table next to him sat three elderly patrons whom Peter could not help but overhear swapping stories of the good old days when a pint was a full pint, and the beer was stout.

Peter listened to their jaundiced reminiscence as the older man spoke his boastful lament. "If I had money, she'd have chosen me. Actors are a selfish and fickle lot."

The younger man nodded amenably, but the poorly clad woman erupted in jaunty laughter. "Your addled in your head. She'd not have had the likes of you. And good too. Consider yourself spared. What with her niece, Aggie, being the undoing of that family. They might have survived some of her antics, but when she popped out the bastard child it all unraveled."

"'Tis true," added the younger man nodding in agreement again.

Curious, Peter interrupted them, "Please forgive, me, but I have been listening. I am sorry. Do any of you know the name Aggie McCallister?"

They all shook their heads mumbling, "No."

"I'm looking for family of a woman, the actress, somewhat as you described. She died, and her son—he was four-or five-at the time—went to a foster home. He would be about 13 or so now. He's a red-headed scamp."

Minds began to calculate as fingers counted out the years

The old lady spoke first, "We don't know no McCallister. But it sounds like Agathe Bancroft. She was an actress well enough. The boy would be about what you say." Turning to her company of friends with a nod, "Twelve or thirteen, right?"

They agreed.

The old man asked, "What's your business with them?"

"Some of the family are looking for them." Peter replied.

He did ascertain the location of the woman's family at Worchester, south of Birmingham. As much as he detested a trip to Worchester, he would still have to go. He might be there for days.

McCallister was a somewhat common name; however, with any luck, he should find a relative or two. Only now he was searching for two names. This was going much too slowly and required a broader net. In each community he placed an advertisement at the local newspaper office. It read:

£100 Reward for certifiable information concerning the whereabouts of one Aggie McCallister or Agathe Bancroft (1811-1844). Contact Peter Fenchyl, 118 Piccadilly, London

CHAPTER VIII

PETER FENCHYL CONTINUES HIS SEARCH

Responses came every week with myriad information, yet none of a personal nature to help him.

The family were actors, including Agathe. During the 1840s they were quite famous from Birmingham to London with their most renowned work *The Dead Heart*. One of their family's finest solo venues was the Hay Market Theater in Birmingham.

The failure of anyone to step forward and claim the reward struck Peter as odd considering their fame. Maybe she wasn't held in high esteem by acquaintances of the time or even her family. Yet in late November 1856, persistence paid off. From the darkness stepped forth a reluctant gentleman, an actor from Birmingham.

They met in Peter's office between Christmas and New Year's late one evening. When Peter answered the door Squire Bancroft introduced himself as her second cousin on her father's side. When they were seated, each with a small glass of brandy, Squire began.

"Mr. Fenchyl, the story is so sordid. It is not likely anyone wants to recall it. I have no interest in your reward, but some good I hope will come of our discussion, else I'll not permit its use. Is that agreeable with you?" Squire spoke it more as a statement than a question.

"Yes, of course. My client has no interest in dredging up the family's past," he replied. "If our investigation proves successful, you will find an extreme deal of pleasure in it."

Squire continued. "So, what I'm about to tell you is mostly second-hand. She was 29 when I was born, so I can't speak firsthand of her early affairs. Agathe was among the most successful actresses in the family. Her unusual beauty charmed the most peered of men. I could go on, but that's another story. Perhaps she found too much fame, too quickly. She married Alastair McDougal. They had no children and divorced. He was quite jealous because she began seeing several men, I'm told. Then she had another go of it—lasted less than a year.

Gin was her downfall, along with the opium smoking. It was the end of a beautiful career and, ultimately, her life.

By the time I was born in '31 she had all but disappeared. She stayed with some Hamsteads at the end.

In hard times she had sold herself to wealthy men, men who only wished for bragging rights. She got herself in the family way. Some thought he was likely aborted, but I know she had a boy when I was eight.

There was talk of finding her child and—after she died, you know. The search lasted about a year before they gave up. My cousin said they'd searched orphanages for him after she died. And no one knew where that Hamstead family went.

Squire took a deep drink of his brandy to punctuate his tale. Squire added, "Yours was a clever thought to draw me out. That idea never came to us."

He took another sip to brace himself for the difficult questions Peter might ask.

Peter wanted to tell Squire the rest of the story and how it turned out well, but remained reticent until facts could be substantiated. He continued sipping his drink contemplating the details, then pushed forward.

"But who was the boy's father?"

"I can't say for myself. You understand?" replied Squire.

"And who will know?" asked Peter pointedly.

Squire was silent for a moment, then responded, "My grandmother, the Baroness of Worchester."

Peter found himself in a sweat, either from the news or the brandy, he wasn't sure. Trying not to rush, Peter calmly asked, "May we approach her?"

"I believe so. I will get word to her that I wish to visit, and bring a friend," he offered.

"Yes, please be in touch when you have a date. I will bear necessary expenses," Peter offered.

As Squire rose he said his goodbyes and departed.

Peter retrieved a letter from Lord Henry inquiring of any progress. Peter posted a letter the same day expressing guarded hope. He told of a longer stay in London that might provide more information. After that, he promised a complete accounting of his work and the information gleaned. He closed his letter personally saying he hoped for another stay at Grafton Forest with his family.

In London, Squire and Peter met for a second time, again at Peter's office.

"I have been reconsidering this plan to visit Grandmama. What will you put her through?" Squire asked. "Is it really necessary that you speak with her?"

"I'm not writing a book about anyone. My client merely wants information relative to his choice in a personal matter."

"I'm sorry, but I don't have a good feeling about this," Squire confessed.

"I need to know the father of her child," Peter reiterated with annoyance.

"Only for what reason?" Squire persisted.

"I cannot say," Peter retorted impatiently.

"You see, without a better explanation, I am concerned about the hurt I may heap upon my family and others as well. No one speaks of it," Squire explained.

For the space of three minutes the two reflected on their wishes and needs. Veracity and clarity were about to come together.

Peter took a page of paper from his desk drawer, dipped his pen into ink, and proceeded to write a at some length. Squire sat patiently, uncertain, but not interrupting Peter finished, silently reread his text and passed it to Squire. "Will this help?" Peter asked.

Contract of Agreement

I agree on my sacred promise that any information provided me by any member of the Bancroft family shall not be shared with any person, save the parties of this agreement, particularly information appertaining to the names or status of the father,_____, and the mother, Agathe Bancroft, of a child christened: _____, born: September, 1839.

In the event of the transmission of information included in this document without the permission of Margaret Bancroft, she shall be paid the sum of £100,000, by authorization of Duke Henry FitzRoy, VII, as a penalty for divulging said information

Dated: Witnessed:

Squire read it several times, feeling better, but would not relent until he had spoken with close members of his family.

"Thank you for reconsidering," replied Peter.

A week later Squire told Peter that Grandmama was willing to see him. She lived in London with her sister. Grandmama was about to turn 79. She had as well been an actress in her day.

Approaching the tenement, Peter experienced a feeling that wouldn't subside. People such as these almost always sought compensation. That wasn't going to happen.

When they knocked on the third-floor door, a frail female voice answered.

"That's Grandmama. She wants us to come on in."

She smiled, greeting the pair, and pointing to the chairs at the lone table near the window.

"I'm Madame Bancroft, and you must be Peter Fenchyl," she remarked. "It is a pleasure to meet you. I understand you're a barrister. How nice."

"It is a pleasure for me to meet you, a successful actress of the Hay Market Theater. How much I heard of it in my youth!"

Grandmama feigned a slight blush and nodded her head.

"You've come to speak of my little Agathe. Our loss was so profound. She was in her prime, sought after by more beaus than we could number. Tell me, please, how I can help you. Are you writing her story? Extolling her great successes?"

"As much as I would like that," Peter smiled warmly, "I'm visiting for another reason. Accordingly, I am seeking her son's father."

A chill settled on the room.

"And why is that?" she coldly inquired as the delight of rekindled fame was dashed.

"The boy would come into wonderous opportunities were he sired by a certain gentleman," Peter answered.

Eavesdropping set aside, a second woman entered the room.

"Oh," Madame Bancroft interrupted. "This is my sister, Charlene. Charlene, this is Mr. Fenchyl. He is inquiring about your niece, Agathe."

Charlene nodded in acknowledgement.

"So, Mr. Fenchyl, how can we help you with your work?" Charlene feigned a polite demeanor.

"I am in need of the name of her child's father," Peter restated.

"Oh, that was so many years ago. As well, she had a number of beaus."

"I believe we are seeking the one she knew over Christmas in 1838. You see, we believe we know the name of the father and date of the child's birth," Peter offered. "I expect between you two fine ladies, she confided in her auntie or grandmother, or her grandmother knew her whereabouts. And if I dare say, we know Agathe was interested in rank, as are most. So, it seems likely he wasn't a common bloke but a fine and perhaps wealthy gentleman," Peter pressed.

The score was 0 to 0. Madame Bancroft, the actress, devised a new script.

"I know someone who can help us. He would be asking for a few quid to make it work. Is your man able to help?" she queried him?

"What do you have in mind?" Peter asked.

"I believe 500 would do it," she responded.

"I would like to counter," offered Peter after a moment's pause. "What would it be worth to the two of you to be reunited with Agathe's son, your great grandson? And to know he is here in London? And to see him at the ripe old age of 17 already marked for success and fame? To attain the love and affection due a grandmother and great aunt? Does this top your bid?"

The ladies' faces turned from sweetness to anger.

"What a wicked thing to do!" spat Grandmama.

As Squire and Peter walked from the building, Squire was quiet initially, but when he could take no more, he stopped abruptly. Confronting Peter directly, he demanded, "Do you know where my nephew is?"

"I do," Peter replied.

"And you won't tell us of him. That seems a dishonorable thing to do to a family."

"I am employed to find information. What my employer arranges following his payment to me is his business. I can tell you that no ill will is intended toward anyone. In the end, you will see that," Peter assured him. "That said, all I need is the name and the location of the father. That's all."

Squire felt relief. He knew some of the answers, but clearly Grandmama must be the one to decide that. After today, he was sure she would.

CHAPTER IX

CECILIA'S HURT WANES, TENDING ELIZABETH

As time and tides wait for no one, at Grafton Manor, life was changing as well.

Thomas turned 20 and forgot Elizabeth; rather, he pursued an older girl, Minnie, much more to his liking. As Horton's right-hand man he enjoyed a taste of power. Horton had had a fall, and Thomas handled most supervisory tasks until Horton was back on his feet.

Elizabeth at 16 had become an assistant to Missus Wallander. She developed a taste for education and completed it in her spare time.

Lord Henry and Lady Cecilia continued to develop their pet project, Grafton Forest. .Its surprising success attracted a large number of the well-to-do and required three more employees.

Midafternoon brought the sound of the knocker on the front door of the manor. Maximillian answered.

"I'm Newton FitzRoy; I wonder if my uncle is at home?" he asked.

"I'll check, sir," he replied.

When he returned, opening the door; he instructed Newton, "Follow me."

Maximillian led the way to Henry's personal library, announcing upon entering, "Sir, your nephew, Newton FitzRoy."

"Newton, it is so nice to have you drop by. I believe it's been a year since last we were together. And, what brings you to our end of the Kingdom," Henry inquired.

"I was in London, and mother said I should see you if I could. So, I took the train to Dover and a short ride by carriage here. Mother heard you had experienced a severe case of arthritis. She wanted to know if you were any better," Newton spoke cordially.

"I'm having considerable trouble with it. My doctor says with medications and rest I should improve soon. However, the manor is doing well.

We have built a new lodge that we let. It's been very successful," Henry told him, "Large numbers can visit for days if they wish."

"As well, Uncle, I wondered if I might be a help to you as you recover? I'm free for a time with nothing to prevent me," Newton generously offered.

Lord Henry sensed in Newton's remarks that he was eager as ever to be considered as an eligible next duke. Henry felt boxed in—that he might be compelled to confirm

Newton as his heir. It would please Newton and his mother, Alyssa.

"I have been giving thought to someone to follow me. I'll not be assured many more years. It is only something I must look into. Would you be interested?" he inquired of Newton, subtly baiting.

"Oh, there is such responsibility," Newton responded in an obsequious tone. "I think, yes, but there is so much to learn before taking on such an opportunity. I'm not yet married; however, it appears I will marry within the year."

"That's good news," Henry replied. "Is she anyone I might know?"

"No, I think not. She is from the Berkshire family of Birmingham."

"Regarding my successor, I have hired Fenchyl, a barrister in London, to help with that. He is having some success he tells me."

"You're saying someone from the family, I suppose?" queried Newton.

"Yes, that's right."

"Are you able to say whom?" Newton ventured.

"No, not at this time. It may be months or hopefully years anyway before that time comes," responded Henry.

Cecilia stuck her head in the doorway, greeting Newton.

"Newton, it's so good to see you. How is Alyssa?" she asked.

"Very well, thank you. She told me to give you a hug for her," Newton said, standing and embracing his aunt.

"I'll ask Missus Wallander to set another place for you at dinner. Won't you stay and join us?" prompted Cecilia.

Newton glanced toward Henry and then back to Cecilia, "Yes, I'd like that, thank you," he responded.

"May I offer you a brandy, Newton?" inquired Henry.

"Certainly, Uncle, I would be most thankful."

With that, they settled into a set of armchairs, discussing recent political unrest and news from the front. At length Maximilian entered and announced, "Dinner is served, your Lordship."

Following dinner, Henry welcomed Newton to stay the night.

"A train leaves Dover at 10:45 in the morning. We will have you taken to the station, and you shall be back in London shortly following midday." Henry offered.

It took little encouragement; Newton would remain the night.

The Hamsteads of Canterbury would occasionally recommend some of the older youth to Lord and Lady FitzRoy. Surprisingly, everyone accepted at the Manor did well in their field of employment and eventually moved on into the community or back to their families. The idea was copied by others to obtain inexpensive help and to provide for orphans. Jenkins added two more rooms to his house to accommodate the increasing numbers.

Laird never wrote to Elizabeth nor she to him, but she listened intently as his letters and exploits were read. The year apart had treated her well. She was thinner and taller and of a fine complexion. Full-grown, she was going to be a beauty, attracting boys as bees at a honeycomb.

Laird was about to complete two years of sea duty on 6 January, 1845. He would come home in December. Then he must return to his ship by 6 February to begin his next year as a cabin boy.

He wondered if the captain was related to the Grafton Manor family since they shared a surname. Consumed by his responsibilities to the captain, he never found the opportunity to ask.

His interest more predominantly turned to attending the Royal Naval Academy in Portsmouth at the first opportunity. There he could begin officer training. From his service aboard the HMS *Beagle*, he obtained a good recommendation from Captain FitzRoy. At his reenlistment, he learned of his reassignment to the HMS *Illustrious*, a two-decker, to begin following his 30-day leave.

It seemed odd to him, but it had been so long since his childhood and seeing his family, that he felt different. He was fully grown now, just over six feet, and was looking to see if he could put Thomas in his place.

He would wear his uniform with its insignias and special battle commendations. He recalled his first day as a cabin boy and all that had transpired with the travels and fighting. He recognized the changes it brought about in him.

Anxious beyond words he signed his request, indicating where he would be if called back before time.

Settled back at home, Laird and Elizabeth were making up for the time apart. They fascinated one another. Laird was impressed that Elizabeth had progressed from kitchen work to assisting Missus Wallander.

Likewise, Elizabeth was in awe of Laird, so much so that she felt the need to restrain herself and the feelings he would afflict her with.

She told him, "This is like seeing a new picture. First, we saw it as a child sees it; now, I see it from an adult's view. It's so much different—so different and so nice."

"That describes it very well. Yet, if you asked me when it happened, I couldn't say. Could you?" he went on.

After just five days at home, they were stealing every opportunity to dart throughout the county, sightseeing in a borrowed curricle.

New to Laird was his need to touch her, maybe to prove she was real. Rather he sensed he had no right to do so, and he put it out of his mind quickly.

Peter didn't know it, but Laird was home with the Hamsteads on leave.

It had been three weeks before Peter heard from Squire. "Grandmama will see you again," he announced with a smile.

"Wonderful," replied Peter. "What time is best?"

"I think midafternoon," Squire replied, "She's at her best in the afternoon. Let's say at two."

"Thank you, thank you, thank you! exclaimed Peter, "I look forward to finishing this soon. I'll be there," he told Squire.

Squire left as quickly as he had arrived.

Thursday at 1:30, Peter made his way to the home of Madam Bancroft's sister on Glenn Avenue, the north side. He was warmly welcomed, and she invited him to join her in the sitting room.

"Welcome," she said with a smile. "Have a seat here next to me so I can hear more clearly."

Peter did so.

"You are correct in your investigation. Agathe was indeed my favorite granddaughter. She was known by almost all of Birmingham. She trusted far too much, and her success became her undoing," she intoned dramatically and paused for the effect.

Then with a turn to practicality she spoke again, "You know of my great-grandson, but you need more information?" And do you know his name? Tell me more about him."

"Yes, Lady Bancroft, all in good time. I have a few questions for you, you see.

In 1838 do you know whom Agathe was seeing?"

"I believe I can help you, but it escapes me just now," she spoke coyly. I know he was a naval officer of some rank. They met in the middle of October at a military ball every year," she answered.

"Were they exclusive with one another?"

"Yes. But he was married and having difficulties. He thought he could clear that up in two or three months. His wife wanted to be free of him. I think because she had other interests as well. Do you know what I mean?"

"Did you know your granddaughter to be pregnant at any time during their relationship?" Peter asked.

"It is still difficult to speak about. She paused, inwardly acknowledging the hurt. "I did know. She told me in January and was concerned they had become intimate too soon. She also wanted to... well, get rid of it, you know," she left off. "The family opposed that, and a quarrel ensued.

She was seriously deciding between her career and a child. Her career was more important at the time. In early February she disappeared. We thought she had run away to get rid of it. Some said first one place and then another. London was the most likely."

Finally she admitted, "I do recall his given name—Robert. She called him Bob. How long before I can see my great-grandson?"

"Yes, of course, but we don't even know where he is exactly. He's in the Navy somewhere. I'm looking for him. When we get more information, this will come together or said another way, we want to be sure Bob is the boy's father. You, see?"

"One moment, please," she begged as she called her sister. "Charlene, will you come here. Please bring me the small case under my bed. With my suitcase likely I can help more. I even know the name of the midwife if you wish," she volunteered freely now.

"While Charlene stepped away, she picked up where she had left off.

"Robert joined us in the search for her. After four months, however, he returned to his position. He was to carry a "Darwin" to a place called Galapagos.

Charlene returned with the case, handing it gently to Lady Bancroft.

"Do you have any written material of Bob's?" inquired Peter after the case was opened.

"I see an envelope where he sent her something, but no letter remains. Here's a list of money I loaned her. She was penniless even before she disappeared. It seemed to me he abandoned her. We think he was grateful she was missing and returned to his family."

Peter was busy making notes.

"May I borrow the envelope?" he asked. "I'll return it after comparing the handwriting."

"I'll make a list of things if you wish," she responded.

"Do you find other information concerning the navy?" he asked.

She sifted through the rest of its contents, finding another envelope with a letter enclosed. On this envelope, he had placed his return address, which included his rank. It indicated he was a lieutenant.

The letter was short. When Peter asked if they might read it, she agreed. It was dated June of '38.

My Darling, Agathe,

I've just returned from the Americas with a hold of walnut wood. The work keeps me on task and spares me thinking of you all the day long. With any good fortune I expect to see you by the first of October.

I trust I am still welcome to stay with you for the two weeks I have ashore.

How was your engagement in Birmingham went. I'm sure you were the darling of all the men in attendance with all the women jealous

I know not that which my wife will surprise me upon return. My barrister tells me he has the means to bring this awful matter to a quick and quiet close with more news from my family.

My father adores you, admitting you're the most beautiful woman he knows. But he abhors that you are in the theatre. About what I think, there is no other man so lucky as me.

I must close for now, saying this: The evening would be grand if you were in my arms.

With all my love,
Bob

The two sat, considering the end of a matter that had gone so wrong.

Grandmama continued, "I tried several times to explain what she was doing was not likely to work out for good. You know, I believe she thought me more than disagreeable and wholly wrong. It violates the laws of God and man to break marriage commitments," she stated with sternness in her voice.

"You have done more to help me than any other lead," Peter uttered.

"And, Peter, you have promised me I will see my grandson soon, yes?"

"Yes," he answered.

He finished his tea and said his goodbye to Madam Bancroft with a slight bow.

Back in his office, Peter sat with his feet on the desk, leaning back with his fingers interlaced behind his head. What was his next step to be? It left no doubt concerning the child's parentage. The navy would be his first stop.

Where the son was, he expected to be easier; he had somewhat of a trail on him already.

CHAPTER X

DUCHESS CECILIA'S SCHOOL FOR GIRLS

At Grafton Manor the Duke was experiencing greater physical problems with his joints. At age 63 he expected some aches and pains, but his physician diagnosed his pain as rheumatoid arthritis. He began to find himself bound to a wheeled chair. Hot baths helped. Opium was used, but his physician advised to use it as little as possible. This condition was to make his final years most difficult.

The Duchess, Cecilia, was well and had found a social cause closer to home that suited her. It was the teaching of girls, a dame's school of sorts. Elizabeth, Mrs. Burton's assistant, caught the eye of Cecilia, who invited her to join in teaching at the school. After several months, it was apparent Mrs. Burton was going to lose good help as Elizabeth was asked to do more in the growing school.

Elizabeth graduated secondary school. She was inspired to help Lady Cecilia start a school as a business. The pair were off to meet Frances Mary Buss, headmistress, who organized the first of such schools in 1850 at the North

London Collegiate School for Girls. Following their meeting, Lady Cecilia became an ardent supporter.

It was a new thing, Lady Cecilia's interest in Elizabeth. Henry noticed. It seemed to Henry Cecilia was recovering from her deep hurt. Elizabeth became her focal point and protégée.

Henry made no mention but was beginning to see Cecilia's eyes brighten. Cecilia felt there wasn't enough that she could do for Elizabeth.

However, educating young women was a cause for conflict. It wasn't a popular matter. It brought derision because young women weren't so quick to marry. That brought a reduction of eligible wives, competition for light jobs, and interference with family life in general. Girls as young as eight or nine were invited. Presently the school boasted five students between 13 and 15.

The curriculum was not so different from other schools, covering mostly the same subjects as secondary schools. Teachers were women who were older, with higher levels of education than was common.

Elizabeth excelled in her studies and in teaching the younger girls. Schooling moved her yet further from Thomas and his farmhand mentality. Because the classroom was in the manor house, she was able to stay on as payment for teaching and helping Duchess Cecilia.

Peter visited Lord Henry at the Manor.

"I have come to report my progress thus far," he told Henry with a bubbly, self-assured look.

"Say on, say on," Henry excitedly begged.

"Your heir lives," Peter blurted. The story is a bit sordid, but your line continues. At your will I can present sufficient information to confirm it. I am yet unable to produce the parties, but I believe that to be the easy part. Your nephew, now the right honorable Admiral Robert FitzRoy, sired a child in 1839. That child is today enlisted in Her Majesty's Navy. He was 17 on his last birthday. I expect your cousin and the boy likely easy to reach as they both serve in the navy," Peter stopped to catch his breath.

Peter took some time to explain what had transpired with the Bancrofts, the years in-between, and the mother's end.

"When I find them, what would you have me do or say?" he asked.

"From what you say, I believe I recall meeting them," continued Henry, "It would have been 30 or so years ago at a stage play in Birmingham. Grandmama was quite an aloof woman."

Henry pondered his next move as he called for tea. "Do you believe we could get them here at the manor and tell them? What manner of child is the son, one of ill-repute or like as unto you?"

"His grandmama presumes him to be the finest of young men; however, she doesn't really know. Do you recall the ginger-headed boy who grew up with the Hamsteads in Canterbury."

"Yes, I recall him because he looks like my family. When I spoke with him the first time, he said to me, in somewhat of a vaunt, 'Lord FitzRoy, pardon my boast, but I know I'm made of finer stuff than this.' Later he told me he didn't like the name Laddie—that he was growing out of it. Wanted to be known as Laird. I thought it a bit odd, but I agreed and wished him well. "

"I will first find Admiral FitzRoy and entreat him with an offer to visit you, not telling him of Laird. I feel sure he will be pleased to see you. I should think he would be with his family during the holidays. I could speak to Jenkins about the lad's whereabouts. At any rate, I'll work to that end, keeping you posted on my success. I'll not make any arrangements without informing you.

"Have you considered my offer of quid pro quo?" Henry prompted?

"I have, and I agree"

Bear in mind the calendar is rather full. Considering your fees, I think you will find ours are equally expensive," Henry replied with a grin.

The next week Peter presented himself in Portsmouth at Her Majesty's naval base. At the desk nearest the entrance, he asked for the office of Admiral Robert FitzRoy.

He was directed by a clerk to the second floor and told, "Turn right about 20 yards. You will see his name on the door."

"Thank you," he intoned as he turned toward viewing the beautiful halls and historical pieces along the way.

When he reached the doorway, he was humbled knowing he was about to visit such a celebrated official. As a professional himself, still, it hadn't occurred to him that he wasn't going to walk right in and greet the admiral. However, upon leaving minutes later, he did have an appointment to meet with a staff person the next afternoon at 3:00. So all was not lost.

He returned to his office in London, working on a number of matters, including dates he wished to reserve the Grafton Forest property for his family's visit.

The next day he arrived somewhat early at FitzRoy's office, announcing his appointment at 3 to the clerk. He was directed to be seated as the clerk contacted the assistant of the admiral.

At 3:15, a short, older man came to him, smiling and extending his hand.

"I'm Lieutenant Granderson. Won't you come with me?" he said as he pointed the direction and then followed Peter.

They entered a fine office where Peter was offered a chair near Lieutenant Granderson's desk. The officer then took his seat.

"I'm Peter Fenchyl, a barrister representing Duke Henry FitzRoy of Grafton Manor."

"And how may I help Duke FitzRoy today, Mr. Fenchyl?"

Peter, sensing the time was short, got right to the point, "The Admiral is Duke Henry's cousin. The duke wishes Admiral FitzRoy to be his guest. Being stricken with age, the duke has private family matters to discuss. And, sir, that is the end of it," Peter concluded.

Granderson wrote his notes in silence.

"Do they know the residence of one another?" Granderson inquired.

"Yes, sir," Peter responded.

"I will see he gets this today. I thank you for conveying his message. Good day."

They rose.

Next, Peter needed the name of Laird's ship and its berthing location. That was harder to gain. In all, it took nearly an hour speaking to four persons to ascertain that the HMS *Illustrious* was the ship and then two more contacts to determine it would be docked at berth number 275, on the Thames, and finally confirmation that the *Illustrious* had put to sea three weeks ago.

Peter was anxious to get back to Lord Henry with the news. The next day he began early, leaving on the 7:00 train and arriving at 11.

Peter and Henry went straight to Henry's private study. Peter held the door as Henry entered and rolled to his desk. Peter was pleased to share his information gleaned at the naval command office.

"From the looks of his suite and staff, I'd say your cousin is a very important man. I didn't see him personally. But from the reaction of Lieutenant Granderson, I believe your invitation will be well received. I expect you will be hearing from him.

It took some extended inquiry, but I found Laird has been transferred to another ship. Presently both Laird and his ship are at sea.

"You do bring good news. Horton told me Laird spent much of his time with Elizabeth and his old friends during shore leave.

The two were often seen around the county together. I didn't expect there would be matchmaking from this. But at my age, I forget some of the old things," Henry said with a smile.

Henry thanked Peter for the news.

"Stay and spend the day. We could go to Grafton Forest. And if it is vacant, we could stay the night. Would you like to inspect it?"

"I would very much like to see the lodge."

"Good; Wellington will assist us."

"You will be needing a horse."

"Yes, that would be wonderful. I play an intense game of chess. Would you care to challenge me?" Peter queried.

"I would."

Henry called for James, the first footman who was passing in the hallway.

"James, will you see Horton about two horses for a trip to the forest, mine and one for Mr. Fenchyl ."

"Yes, milord." And he was gone.

"Cecilia, dear, are you nearby?" Henry called with a raised voice.

"Yes," she returned his call.

"Peter and I will go to the lodge for the night.

He has agreed to reduce our expense for legal work if we provide his family with the use of Grafton Forest. Isn't that nice, dear?" he said to her.

At the front of the manor Thomas stood holding the reins of the horses. Henry was indeed hard-pressed to walk about the barns, but riding, was still a joy. His Lipizzaner, his dear old friend, was showing more white hairs in his coat.

Cecilia could be heard from the doorway, "Try not to drink too much, dear. Peter, watch out for him."

The narrow roadway was vibrant with sounds of the forest as they made their way to the lodge. It made for an enjoyable late afternoon ride.

CHAPTER XI

NEWTON FITZROY REMAINS AN
AVAILABLE HEIR

The *Illustrious*, originally due back in August, was delayed three months. The news brought many a heavy heart, including Laird's. To Laird it passed quickly though because he was at sea. To those who had plans and intentions, such as Peter, Henry, and Elizabeth, it seemed his time away would never end. He continued at the rank of Boy 1 and engaged in several skirmishes, the most difficult being Ireland. Many wished for home rule. They were Republican Separatists. Laird considered Scotland and Ireland a part of his own country, England, and so, sadly, he must be a belligerent against them.

Their present orders were to carry British troops to quell the uprising in Ireland. During the skirmish, small arms fire came upon the *Illustrious* from the rebels trying to drive them away. The rebels resented the British sticking their noses into Irish affairs.

To the gun deck Laird brought powder and shot for the crew when he struck his thigh on a carlin. Thinking nothing of it, he continued trips to the magazine with a slight limp.

By mid-afternoon Laird's right leg began to ache more intently. He took some time to see to it. Considerable moisture had accumulated in the boot.

The blood brought panic and a cry, "Get me a medic, please." In minutes a soiled old man attended him. "Let me see it," he ordered and cut Laird's pant leg just below the buttock. Wiping away the blood and digging around, the medic announced, "Man, you've been shot. The ball is more than halfway through your thigh. It's got to come out and soon, or it'll go to blood poison." Laird had nothing to say. The words in his head were better left unsaid.

Laird was carried to the infirmary. In ten minutes he was on the table, the utensils sterilized and laid out.

The medic reiterated, "The ball went aways into your leg. Fortunately, it missed the bone by a hair's width. We'll find it and then clean it up," the old salt said. Following a good washing with whiskey, and a half glass for Laird, a piece of leather was placed between his teeth. A prod was inserted.

The captain, hearing of injuries to the crew, pulled the *Illustrious* back several yards and waited for dark for troops to reapproach the shore unseen.

A few moments in, moisture was dripping from Laird's eyes to his ears and then to the table as he growled ugly sounds.

The medic was quick and within minutes he handed Laird the mini ball as a keepsake. The wound was swabbed with whiskey several times over again and a patch placed over it.

Laird was off his feet for two days before going to a crutch. By the end of four weeks, he was just about back to himself.

He had missed little. The marines were put ashore during the early hours and then the ship put quietly back to sea, a hold full of ordnance on the way to the British in southern Ireland.

Mid-September of '57, Newton paid another unannounced visit to Grafton Manor. Without being obvious, he wanted to know if Uncle Henry was any closer to naming an heir to the dukedom.

Henry was indeed physically much worse, unable to move alone from his chair any longer.

"I wanted to stop in to inquire if you are doing better. I am very sorry to see that you are not," sympathized Newton.

"My condition seems to come and go. As I'm sure you can imagine, I must be careful always. It seems you are one of the fortunate ones," Henry replied.

I continue to serve mother in her affairs. She will be 57 soon, you know, and is doing quite well."

"Cecelia will be pleased with the news. She has spoken to me about visiting London to see Alyssa. I may not be able to go with her, however," Henry replied, casually pointing at his chair.

Newton queried, "Peter tells me he believes he has found a candidate. Have made progress locating a successor?

"We will know soon," Henry replied.

"Speaking plainly, I should be honored with the position. I think myself fortunate my condition is no worse. Concerning my credentials, I believe myself to equal anyone in the field," Newton spoke with all the humility he could muster.

Henry responded, "Yes, I'm sure that's true." True or no, Henry felt something lacking and didn't encourage Newton.

It was not to be the end of Newton's compunction to worm his way into Grafton Manor. Time after time, he and his mother had been rebuffed in no uncertain terms. He could not let it go.

His mother's estate and Henry's manor would be something of which to boast throughout all of England. Power and wealth would be his. So much so that he could feel the pride of it all even now. But how? There must be some way.

At Portsmouth Naval Command, Admiral FitzRoy examined his schedule for an opportunity to visit his cousin at Grafton Manor. The time between Christmas and New Year's might be best. He was sure cousin Henry and Cecilia would have a New Year's party. With the dignitaries in attendance, it might present itself as a good time to become better acquainted in his bid for Prime Minister.

He considered the timing for two days before committing it to a letter to Henry. He apologized for any inconvenience, but it would have to be over the holidays. He would be accompanied by two lieutenants when he traveled. It would be a privilege for them to be with a family during the holidays.

Lieutenant Granderson posted the letter. Only thrice in 25 years had Robert visited. Henry thought it was because

Robert wished for the dukedom. But Robert had succeeded in every way: a fine family of four daughters, a career ranked near the highest command of the navy, and travel around the world enjoying sights few see. Henry had always admired his cousin. But Robert seemingly never felt the same.

Peter feared some conflict between the two cousins. Hard feelings might surface, but securing an heir was the most important thing to Henry.

Thursday evening, in London, Peter rounded the corner of Air and Piccadilly, returning to his office to gather a file for a pleading the next morning. He must be in court before 10.

Piccadilly Circus was among the first to have whale oil lights, and lamplighters were making their rounds at the circus as Peter approached his building. The lights did little good but were somewhat of an improvement in the deepness of night.

In his second-floor office window on the left he detected a soft glow. To his surprise, he found his door open a half an inch. He stopped, suspicious that his clerk may have left the door unsecured. But that wasn't likely.

His second concern regarded an intruder. He waited and listened. Yes, he heard a desk drawer open. Just inside on the left was a cricket bat leaning against a cabinet. Its purpose was to bring order if needed.

Leaning, stomach against the door frame, he inserted his right arm, feeling for the bat. With the bat in his right hand, he used the left to slowly push the door open enough to see a shadowy figure with a small lamp rummaging through cabinets. At the right moment, he squeezed through the partially open door watching the intruder.

After collecting himself, he spoke in a clear and commanding voice, "Friend, can I help you find something?"

Shocked, the intruder spun around, garbled something, and stood paralyzed facing the figure of a man at the door holding a cricket bat.

After an extended moment, Peter spoke again demanding, "Who might you be?"

It appeared the man wanted a way out, but Peter and the bat gave him no opportunity.

"I'm Newton. I can see I've come to the wrong office. It's my uncle's office I wanted. I have erred. I mean you no harm," Newton added. "I merely needed to retrieve papers for my uncle."

"I don't feel so confident of that. Perhaps we should locate a peeler to investigate the matter in which we find ourselves. What do you think? Will you kindly turn your lamp up so I can see you better, and you me? Our positions aren't likely to change until we enjoy a little more clarity. Don't you agree?" asked Peter.

"I'm Peter Fenchyl. This is my law office. I am guessing you are Newton FitzRoy, and your uncle is Henry. Am I correct? I do have your uncle's file. What might you wish from it?"

When the lamp was turned up, the disheveled room confirmed Newton's guilt.

"What say we come clean and not have a peeler involved? No one's been murdered, and no harm has been done but to muss up my office. I know I would prefer to conclude it that way," Peter suggested as he sat on the edge of a table, bat still in hand.

Newton was reluctant as he stuttered and stammered meaningless words about something that wasn't fair. He then sat in Peter's chair.

With more calm now Newton began, "I know of you. My Uncle Henry hired you to find some of our family. Due to his condition, he is searching for a man to follow him. I believe it should be me." Newton insisted.

"Really? He should choose a common burglar such as yourself," Peter pointed out.

"I've spoken to him several times about it. He doesn't say it, but he thinks hemophilia disqualifies me. That's not right," Newton said bitterly.

"I believe I better understand," replied Peter, "You are man enough to know we are often dealt cards hurtful to us. Your condition for example."

Peter continued, "I think I know who the new duke will be. As well, you are correct; it shan't be you.

And what if you knew? Would you harm him to improve your chances? Can you not see that to remain in your uncle's good graces is better than being cut from his will altogether? Only you can know the pain of your circumstances, but isn't it better to bear up as a good man and your integrity remain intact?"

Newton remained quiet, anger bubbling.

"Why don't we just return to our homes, and this never be mentioned," Peter prompted. "With one exception. After my clerk cleans this up, I would ask you to reimburse me for the expense. Is there anything more I can help you with concerning your uncle?"

Newton considered Peter's admonition and the logic thereof. His feelings continued to boil, but to pursue it would cost him so much more.

"No. I apologize for my actions. My address is 2394 Bullsmoor Lane in Birmingham. I shall pay for the mess. It is clear why Uncle Henry engages you. I shall remember and call on you if the need arises. May we close our meeting and return home?" Newton entreated.

"Yes," Peter said as he crossed the room to shake Newton's hand. "Oh, I almost forgot to invite you to the dinner at your uncle's on New Year's Eve. You will meet the soon-to-be duke.

I guarantee you will be surprised by the dignitaries, announcements, and appointments that evening. Cecilia will send invitations, so tell your mother. I need to remain here to prepare a pleading—if I can find it in this mess—for the morning."

Newton, saying, "Goodnight," left freely on his way to his quarters in London.

CHAPTER XII

A BAD APPLE IS PLUCKED FROM THE BARREL

Newton had seen in Peter's papers the name of the man Peter sought, Laird Hamstead, a navy man. It didn't make sense. This Hamstead was the target of Peter's search, but Newton saw no logical reason for it.

Newton made more trips to Peter's office undetected and discovered Hamstead was thought to be a FitzRoy. He couldn't see the connection, but it was evident to him it was so. He had found Hamstead's ship's name and berth number as well.

What if Hamstead were to vanish? What if, in the end, there were no FitzRoys but himself?

Over the next week, Newton devised one plan and then another. Finding the ship and the man seemed easy, rather like a puzzle, but he couldn't put it together alone.

The underbelly of London was comprised of people who could make things happen. From Birmingham to London there was a group known to make people disappear and the like. They were referred to as the Castle Gang. It was risky to get others involved. It would also be costly.

Following ten days of leaving 'help wanted' notes at dozens of pubs, there came a knock at Newton's door.

Alyssa answered it. She was taken aback by the rough figure who asked if Newton were there.

"Yes, but can I help you," she asked, "I'm his mother."

"No, Lady, I need to see him," the man replied.

"Okay, I'll get him. Will you wait out here?" she asked.

He didn't answer, and she left him there. When she located Newton she said, "Son, there's a stranger wanting to see you."

Newton and the man walked away from the house front and began speaking. His mother couldn't hear. The man handed Newton a posted paper. Newton struggled with where to begin, asking, "Does Castle mean anything to you?"

"And if it does, what's it to you?" the stranger responded tersely.

"I have a tough job. I need a tough person to handle it," spoke Newton with feigned confidence. "Can you make someone disappear?"

The man looked Newton in the eye and said, "For the right price, I can do anything. I know Castle. What are we talkin' 'bout?"

"There's this guy I want gone in a few days. How much?" Newton asked.

"Depends on how difficult, but we'll start at £500, depending on if it's easy or not. I'll tell you when I know. Don't worry; you can afford it."

"I don't wish to kill him, just see he never returns to London again," Newton said.

"When I'm ready, I'll come back for half the money. Who is he, and where do I find him? It'll be a day or two to size him up."

Newton gave him Laird's name, the ship's name, and its berthing location. It had returned only days before from Ireland. Newton asked, "What's your name, so I'll know you?"

"You don't need my name. We'll always do business right here at your home; the fewer people involved, the better," he replied.

"Man, you're out of your head. At midnight you think I have £500 in my nightgown pocket for you? You can't be serious!" Newton spoke vociferously, then remembered his mother. Once again, in a whisper, he offered, "Right now?"

With no emotion the man demanded, "Is it a yes, or no?"

Uncertainty plagued Newton. What was he about to do, but he spoke the words, "Okay, okay, I'll be right back. Wait here,"

When Newton returned he hissed, "I don't have it all. I'll give it to you when you return with your report."

Five days following, the stranger returned near midnight. A rapping at the front door of Alyssa's home called Newton to respond. He went down to find the stranger.

"Do you know what time it is?" demanded Newton in an irritated tone.

The man ignored his protest.

"This is the deal; it's arranged. We will begin when you pay me £500. The price is £750. I will return to collect the other when we have completed our job."

It was ten minutes before Newton returned with the money. The man took it from him. Turning to go, Newton stopped him with a question, "Excuse me, don't I get a receipt or something?"

The stranger stepped into the street, saying as he went, "What are you thinkin'? I'm a bloody bank or somethin'?" He disappeared into the darkness of the night.

Two days later Laird was celebrating at home with friends. In the morning, with his sea bag, he boarded the train to Portsmouth.

Three days later, his failure to report aboard the *Illustrious* was evident.

He was so near the completion of three years of sea duty. Following that and the holidays, he would be headed to Great Britain's Naval Training Center, if all went well.

On the prior Saturday evening, Laird had been returning to his ship late and in a tipsy condition. Two men wrestled him to the ground, tied and gagged him, and put a blindfold about his head. They led him through the back streets of Portsmouth.

The assailants stopped for the space of an hour or so, then continued. Assured of his confusion, his captors took him to the wharf. Laird knew the sound of water lapping against a ship, but it was no help.

A third man had joined as Laird could hear three whispering. Then he was jostled forward with the softly spoken command, "Hold the back of my shirt and stay close; otherwise, you'll fall and drown."

He discerned that he was being led aboard a vessel on a narrow gangplank. When they reached the deck, he was half-dragged through the hold, which smelled of livestock, except there were voices and other sounds of men. Slaves! They were slaves; he was sure of it.

Likely they were outbound, so it seemed to him. He recalled outbound slaves were taken to the Caribbean.

Panic began to smother his soul.

"What are you doing with me?" demanded Laird, but no response was forthcoming, and the gag was tightened.

A short time later he could hear the sounds on deck and the movement of the crew.

In minutes he could feel the motion of the ship; they were leaving the dock. He knew the smell of profuse sweating as they made their way through the cargo of men, likely black men. The stench was overwhelming. As the cargo was commonly set midship, it seemed they might be moving toward the bow or somewhere near the head.

When they stopped, he was told to kneel down. There came a foot from somewhere that pushed him into something of a closet. With his feet and hands tied; a canvass was thrown over him.

It was quiet, other than the creaking of the ship and the occasional moan of a slave. He listened to interpret every sound. He knew they were gone, and he was, only God knew where, alone.

The ship was underway as he began considering his plight.

After an indeterminate number of hours, he found a rough timber and began the process of cutting away the ropes on his hands. It was a day and night before he freed his hands. Next to come off was the blindfold. Visually he knew where he was. Just as he thought, near the head. Next was the gag in his mouth.

As he worked to untie his feet, his mind raced for the next step.

Someone on board had participated in his kidnapping. Whom could he trust? Who would do him harm?

What to do—what to do! The person least likely to be an enemy should be the captain. That seemed reasonable. He considered how to get to the other end of the ship without being seen.

A steep set of stairs near the first mate's quarters was found on most vessels. If he should stay below and make his way carefully to those stairs and then up, he could reach the captain. He would have to pass through the crew quarters as well but didn't expect anyone to be awake there. Even if someone was, it was too dark to see faces.

When? He had to think about that next.

The very early morning seemed best. The crew would still be in their hammocks and the slaves asleep as well. It would be the next morning. Sleep that night was somewhat better as he was free of his bonds.

When he awoke, there was no light of day that he could tell. Other than a few groans from slaves, all seemed good for his attempt. He stood, stretched to get his limbs moving once more, and slowly crept from the small space onto the flooring of the hold. He reeked from urine during his confinement.

Carefully he felt his way along, row by row until out of the slave compartment. Next was the crew quarter. A small light hung at the far end of the room. Normally there would be a night watch, but he saw none and quietly made his way to the light. A man stirred and rolled over. Laird stopped, waiting for additional movement, and then hurried through the hallway and onto the stairs.

At the top of the stair he opened the creaking door slowly, peeking to see what lay ahead. Another small light was mounted on the corridor wall.

Beyond it on the left a few feet, was a cabin identified as First Mate.

He wanted the captain, but the first mate would do. When trying to open it, he found it locked and began a light rapping. After a few moments, he heard stirring.

He knocked once more; the door opened a crack, and the surprised first mate appeared.

"I need help. I've been kidnapped and stowed in the head until I just freed myself."

The officer seemed puzzled until he could get his senses and replied, "Is this a joke?" However, after perceiving Laird's general condition and the stench, he was soon convinced.

The officer grabbed items of clothing, offering, "Here. Go clean yourself and come back."

"I can't do that; one of them that kidnapped me is among the crew."

"Confounded!" the officer spat. "Well then clean yourself here in the hall the best you can and put these on. I'll have to wake the captain. Stay by my door in the hallway." He moved on down the passageway to the stern.

Laird hurried to do as he was told, finding the clothing too large. He stood by the door as instructed.

When the first mate returned, he beckoned for Laird to follow him to where they entered the captain's quarters.

At the sight of the captain, Laird snapped to attention, saluted, and spoke, "Sir, I am seaman Laird Hamstead of the *Illustrious*. Saturday night last, I was assaulted, bound, gagged, and blindfolded, and then brought aboard this vessel. They stowed me still bound and gagged in the head. One of your crewmen helped them take me aboard, but I didn't see anyone or hear them speak. After these two days I was able to free myself." He stopped for the captain's response.

The captain mumbled to himself as he called a cabin boy to retrieve coffee for the three.

Laird could see displeasure in the first mate's face.

"You're aboard the *Florentine*, a commercial vessel. And I am Captain Demby."

The captain explained they were bound for the Carribean with slaves then on to Virgina in America. They would return to England with a load of prime Virginia oak, a very costly wood. They were expected back in Portsmouth by the end of November.

The captain offered that if Laird would throw in with them and work for his keep, he would be sure to provide him a letter and stipend like the other men. As far as the unknown kidnapper on board, Laird would have to look after himself.

There was nothing Laird could do but agree. He wasn't going to get a free ride. Laird would have to try to ferret out the kidnapper. He also worried what the captain might do. Leave him in the Caribbean if he should survive the balance of the trip? He would watch for anyone who had a certain interest in him, be it good or bad.

To Laird's good fortune, within a week a British man-o-war was sighted on the horizon, headed for England all supposed. The captain sent a man aloft to send a message to her by semaphore flags. The signal read, "All stop."

When confirmation was received, the two approached. A ship-to-ship transfer line was strung, and Laird was transferred to the navy ship with his letter for Captain Meriweather from Captain Demby.

Following the arrival of the *Bastion* at Portsmouth, gossip flew. Laird's name had been published in the *Daily Telegraph*, causing him much grief when he learned of it. He wasn't drunk. Neither did he desert.

The article brought a good deal of humor among his friends. Two particular men, however, found no humor in it whatsoever. One was Peter Fenchyl and the other Newton FitzRoy.

Nevertheless, it made good print at the time.

DRUNKEN SAILOR BOARDS WRONG SHIP
Laird Hamstead, a seaman of Her Majesty's Navy, boarded the wrong ship and was on his way to the Americas when apprehended mid-Atlantic, where he was transferred to *HMS Bastion* and promptly arrested. He was returned to Portsmouth for trial.

Captain Hamilton, an officer of the military courts, convened the court-martial three weeks following Laird's return. While awaiting trial, Laird was confined to the brig.

Following preliminary information, Laird was asked to relate his experience. The four justices sat in rapt attention.

"I was assigned to go to Ireland, sir, aboard the HMS *Illustrious*, serving with Captain Meriweather." He continued retelling his mishap in lurid detail.

"I wouldn't desert no matter what, sir," Laird humbly concluded to the court. Captain Demby will tell you I was aboard the *Florentine* with him."

After Laird's presentation, the jurists with the evidence left the room to ponder the matter. In just twenty minutes they returned with a verdict.

"Hamstead, we have found you not guilty. Yours is a most interesting story. You are free to go."

So, five weeks after being returned to Portsmouth, he was put aboard a troop transport and returned to the HMS *Illustrious* and the Irish waters of the Celtic Sea once more.

In days another trial commenced concerning Newton FitzRoy. Peter believed it highly likely Newton was responsible for the recent murder of Terrence Youngblood in an effort to cover up his part in the kidnapping of Laird. It was difficult to lay such a charge on a client's family, yet all the pieces fit. He had reported his suspicion to Scotland Yard detectives along with the pertinent information he held. An arrest was made and trial about to begin.

On October 2nd in London, Tresslyn Youngblood, the brother of the murdered Terrence, was seated in the witness box. His testimony was being heard by the *Chancery Division Court*.

According to Tresslyn, his younger brother had been murdered by Newton FitzRoy.

The solicitor continued with questions.

"Did your brother Terrence tell you on the evening of the 23rd that he was going to pay a visit on Mr. FitzRoy the next morning."

"Yes, he had struck a deal with FitzRoy and had collected all but £250."

"Was that the last time you saw your brother alive?"

"Yes."

"Mr. Youngblood, you may stand down. Thank you."

"I now call Missus Leroy to the stand."

"Missus Leroy?" called the solicitor once more.

A frumpy woman in her forties came forward and entered the box, seating herself.

"Good afternoon, Missus Leroy. I will take you back to 24 March, in the morning, rather early. Were you in the scullery preparing breakfast for the FitzRoy house?"

"Yes, sir," she replied.

"Will you tell us what you observed that morning?" he prompted.

"Well, sir, it were a bit foggy, but I could clearly see two men about 10 yards from the house. They was tense with one another like to arguing. The one were a stranger to me, the other being Mr. FitzRoy.

I was working when I heard what I first thought to be thunder. I didn't think nothin' of it. But the next time I passed the window, only Mr. FitzRoy was there. He was looking around for I don't know what. He had something in his hand, but I couldn't see it clearly. He stowed it in his pocket. Then he surprised me when he came into the house through the scullery—he lookin' like he'd seen a ghost. I was inclined to ask him if something were wrong, and I did ask him if I could wrap his injured arm. But he were out and gone before I could say anything.

"Thank you, Missus Leroy. You are excused," instructed the defense solicitor.

She left the witness box returning to her seat.

The solicitor for Newton FitzRoy invited him to the stand, whereupon he came forward.

"Mr. FitzRoy were you on the grounds as Missus Leroy indicated that morning?"

"Yes, sir, I was. That's my home," offered Newton.

"And, did you and Mr. Youngblood have a disagreement?"

"Yes. He was threatening to blackmail me concerning an arrangement we had. I was giving him what for, and he left."

"What did you have in your hand?"

"My pipe."

"What arrangement did you make with the deceased?"

"I'd rather not say, sir. It was a private matter."

"I know," came a loud shout from the gallery.

It was Tresslyn.

"Who said that?" demanded the judge, "Stand up."

Tresslyn Youngblood, in a rage, jumped to his feet.

"You are out of order, sir!" shouted the judge. "I find you in contempt of court. If you have something to say, share it first with a solicitor."

"The court will stand in recess until nine tomorrow. Dismissed," the judge spat and left the bench.

The solicitor for the prosecution rushed to reach Youngblood. Upon finding him in the outer hall, he asked, "Why didn't you share this with me?"

After being seated, Wilber requested, "Okay, let's just pick it up from the beginning."

"My brother was a member of the Castle gang. Weeks before, he told me he had a big one worth £750," volunteered Youngblood. "This wealthy man were paying to have someone kidnapped and taken from England but not to hurt him. The kidnapped man found his way back to London, and this FitzRoy didn't want to pay the last £250 because he had returned. Terrence shouted at him, "It weren't his fault this guy came back somehow. So, when Terrence demanded his money, FitzRoy killed him to cover himself."

The trial concluded with no murder conviction against Newton. It was self-defense because Terrence had struck him with a blackjack, breaking Newton's arm. At the conclusion of the trial, Newton was sent to an Australian prison colony with a 20-year sentence for the kidnapping.

CHAPTER XIII

THE JOY THAT COMETH IN THE MORNING

Peter had sent a post to Squire, inviting both him and his grandmama to the holiday dinner. Peter included Squire's aunt as well.

Unknown to anyone except the Hamsteads, Laird had completed his three-year service requirement three weeks early and was now in a position to begin his Naval Academy schooling in February.

He was content to stay home or enjoy Elizabeth's company. Only once did he see the Weatherfords and that for less than an hour. He and Tom visited twice. Their feelings about one another were changed. They were no longer combatants, but rather friends. Tom had married Minnie six weeks earlier.

Laird spent many hours with Elizabeth over the next several days. She was so different, he thought. Something new was happening; his attraction to her was growing. The next two months were hard to get through.

Henry felt remorse for Newton's fate, and particularly the hardship it was to the family. Cecilia assured Henry all would be well. No ill will had been intended toward Newton. And Cecilia herself did her best to comfort Alyssa.

In early December, Laird received a letter from Peter. He didn't know Peter except that he was a barrister. The letter advised Laird he was invited to the New Year's Eve' festivities. Laird read that part twice more, then reviewed the address to confirm it was indeed to him.

It continued, instructing him to wear his finest dark blue woolen uniform and flat round hat, with the ship ribbon hung from it, his commendations, his rank, an able seaman now, and his Victoria Cross and ribbon, for his injury in Ireland.

Laird gave it to Mary to read to see what she thought. She was beside herself with confusion. Could this be a prank? Mary gave it to Jenkins. They all considered it legitimate.

The thought of attending brought Laird to a cold sweat. He was apprehensive, as fearful as he had ever been at sea. The close of the letter informed him Elizabeth would be invited as well. They were asked to arrive at eight on the thirty-first of December.

When Elizabeth heard the news from Laird, she exclaimed, "I'm not going! I have nothing to wear for such things, and they will be making jest of me."

She confided with Cecilia her reservations while at school the next day.

"Oh, you mustn't think like that. I know what it is, and you will be so pleased. No one will make jest of you, I promise. Do you believe me?" She hurried right over any chance for Elizabeth to respond.

"As for a dress, stay at the house after school tomorrow, and I'll have my maid lay out some selections. Elizabeth, I know you both are concerned, but honestly, there's no reason to be," she assured.

"Consider how you and Laird have proven yourselves. Set aside your concerns and follow my advice," Cecilia entreated.

The words of assurance were shared by Elizabeth with Laird. They were reluctant but agreed to attend.

At 10 a.m. on the morning of the 23rd, three officers of the Royal Navy stepped from the train in Dover. The younger men picked up their bags, and Benert recovered the Admiral's. Soon they were off on the short ride to Grafton.

When the coach pulled to the front door of the manor, Brewster stood in the foreground with Missus Wallander. James, the first footman, stood at attention just behind them. James advanced to open the door of the coach, while Brewster boomed a resounding, "Welcome to Grafton, sirs.

The duke apologizes for not greeting you personally; his legs are troubling him today. James will escort you to your rooms to settle in and freshen up. The Duke will see you, Admiral FitzRoy, at your convenience; ring when you wish."

The guests followed James as Brewster went to the drawing-room to advise Lady Cecilia of the admiral's arrival.

A short while later Brewster observed Henry and the admiral, in Henry's library, bringing one another up to date on each other's affairs.

"They have promoted me from my ship," Robert lamented with exasperation. "Her Majesty has taken me from my fine ship, the *Beagle*, to a beautiful desk that will not float a wit."

"Time doesn't treat us well at all," Henry commiserated, "I have been in this chair now for 18 months with no likelihood of escaping it."

"So, do tell me for what you would have me here?" requested Robert.

"So, would prefer a dukedom to a desk?" Henry chided lightly. I am sure you wouldn't care for the position, would you?"

Robert guffawed. "Not at all. As a young man, you knew I had visions of it, but now I'm sure I've chosen the better."

"I have two family members who qualify. One, unfortunately is in Australia.

"You don't mean Newton do you? Alyssa and Montgomery's boy? What's his business there?" inquired Robert.

"It's a sad affair, but he is a criminal," Henry reluctantly shared.

A look of shock came over Robert's face. When no further comment was made by Henry, Robert chose not to inquire further.

Henry continued, "The other, you shall meet on New Year's Eve'. I should like your assessment of him at that time," Henry stated. "He is young but has FitzRoy blood. That's why I want your approval in the matter. You can do that, I'm sure, won't you?"

"Certainly. If you have nothing more for me, I should like to see your new property. Can you spare me two horses?" Robert requested. "I shall take one of my security detail along."

"Absolutely," encouraged Henry, "I will have Horton bring them round. I would love for you to see it."

At five when school was dismissed Elizabeth and Cecilia delighted in wading through yards of satins and silks searching Cecilia's wardrobe for the perfect gown for Elizabeth.

Cecilia hadn't considered it, but her heart was softening concerning children, and Elizabeth was a joy to work with. She didn't see it yet, but she very much liked helping Elizabeth. In fact, it warmed her heart when she had the opportunity to be there for Elizabeth. Others saw it, but no mention was ever made.

Katherine, Cecilia's maid, assisted the pair. Besides a gown there were shoes, jewelry, and hair combs to consider. Elizabeth was a fair featured girl, nearly 18, so it took little to embellish her form.

Cecilia had told Elizabeth that she and Laird would be presented together. Her excitement about the dinner notwithstanding, she longed to see Laird in his handsome navy uniform of blue wool. To her, his rank of able seaman was significant, as though he were a lieutenant or higher.

The clear and sunny New Year's Eve' Day was cold, an encouragement to the workers to return to the barn as quickly as possible. And the household staff had completed most of their preparation days ahead.

But the party would keep them all busy throughout the day and into the wee hours of the morning. The great hall table was set for 36 guests. The list and seating arrangements were complete.

Such guests as the admiral were seated near the middle. Henry and Cecilia were at opposite ends. Six footmen would attend them, and Maximillian the butler, like the maestro of the orchestra, would oversee the entire occasion ensuring that it played with grace and pomp.

Guests began arriving at a quarter past five. They milled around in the library, sitting room, and anterooms until dinner was announced by Maximillian at five forty-five when a small bell was struck.

As they entered the great hall with its two steps downward, Maximillian announced each guest with their titles. Then came Peter Fenchyl arm in arm with Grandmama Bancroft. Their seeming insignificance garnered little attention.

Two couples later were two new faces to the group, Miss Elizabeth Hamstead, on the arm of Seaman First Class, Laird Hamstead. They were seated, one on each side of Lord Henry.

Lady Bancroft at the far end of the table saw the young couple and felt a rush as her heartbeat more quickly, but she said not a word. They were attractive, but strangers to her.

Lord Henry stood, leaning somewhat against the table's end with a glass in hand, thanked them, and offered a toast.

"To our notable guests, good friends, our family. We are honored to have you in our home this last evening of the year. And in the hope that the coming year will bring us much health and happiness."

With numerous 'Hear, hears,' they all tipped their glasses.

Following the toast, the din of the room drowned out meaningful table conversation. They were jovial, and the wine flowed.

An hour later, following dinner, most had found places to rest or danced with the orchestra's endless melodies from familiar composers such as Bach and Mozart.

As it neared eight, Henry spoke to Peter to seek out Laird, and while he himself would get his cousin's attention. They would meet in Henry's study.

"Keep Laird outside until I call your name. Then bring him in," Henry instructed.

"Very good," replied Peter.

Henry interrupted Robert, saying, "Robert, we have need to go to my study. I have something I must show you."

"Right now?" Robert questioned in annoyance.

"Yes, right now. It won't keep," Henry persisted.

Reluctantly Robert entered Henry's office, poured himself a small drink, and was seated.

Henry poured three more drinks and sat across from Robert, with a drink in hand.

Robert wondered at the extra two glasses but was sure there was a good reason.

Henry was nervous, and his voice gave it away as he squeaked out, "Peter."

The door opened. Peter stepped in first, with Laird right behind him, sporting beads of sweat on his now crimson face. Robert was curious but withheld his questions.

Peter was seated as Laird alone remained standing. Now, looking at one another, Robert and Laird's eyes became fixed, each upon the other's.

"Sir," Laird spoke and continued to stand, saluting but as still and strong as a ship's mast.

"Hamstead, what in blazes have you to do with this matter? I am finding you in the most unusual places," he remarked.

"I know not, sir," Laird nervously replied.

Laird looked next at Lord FitzRoy, then to Peter before locking his eyes once more on the Admiral.

This was Henry's cue.

Henry rolled his chair between Laird and Robert where they stood. Reaching for their hands, he clasped them together, wrapping his around theirs. He cleared his throat, and in a deeper tone now, slowly and solemnly proclaimed, "Father, behold thy natural blood son," he said to Robert looking him in the eye. And without pausing for breath, he then turned, looking to Laird's ashen face and said, "Son, behold thy natural blood father."

Henry observed Robert. Stunned, Robert lost his composure, allowing his empty glass to tumble to the tabletop, breaking. It went no better for Laird. He trembled and wobbled somewhat. And with his jaw-dropping, he placed three fingers on the top of the desk to steady himself. In his head it was as though he wasn't sure what he had heard, nor understood the meaning of it at all.

"Laird," Henry insisted, "take a seat before you lose your balance."

"Yes, sir," and Laird did, thankfully, as his feelings drained him of all coordination.

He continued somewhat incoherently, "Kindly intended, sir, I know my beginnings, Captain, eh..., sorry, Admiral, and you're not a part of it, sir. I barely remember my poor, dying mother."

Henry pushed a half-filled glass to Laird, "Here, sip on this," he instructed, "It will help."

Laired gulped at it.

No one spoke as each considered how time and circumstance had had their way with them, all-be-it, unknowingly. It took time to think and draw from the past, understanding it and its ramifications today.

Laird still couldn't wrap his mind around it. He felt he dishonored his mother in some way he could not yet comprehend.

Robert was first to ask a question when he stuttered, "Henry, did you know Laird enlisted nearly four years ago as a cabin boy aboard the *Beagle*?"

"No, I didn't know that. How interesting. Was he a credit to his position?"

He was my right hand for two years," Robert stumbled with his words. "He was recently kidnapped and halfway to the Americas before being apprehended and charged with being a deserter."

"I am stunned by the knowledge you two have known one another through the Navy," interjected Henry.

Henry explained, "You see Peter and I have searched for more than a year. It began when I hired Peter to find a worthy man to fill my shoes, family, blood and all."

"Along the way, Peter found one thing and then another. I somewhat understand your surprise, and I am just as amazed," continued Henry, "I'm sure it hurt to lose Agathe.

It is a different matter though, finding such a son as Laird whom you didn't know you had, adding joy to joy. It is beyond my comprehension. I know the pain of losing sons, but I know not the joy of sharing my life with a son.

So, beyond that, there are many questions to be asked and answered by the both of you."

Laird remarked, "I've always admired you, sir. As a son, it takes me to a whole new place of admiration. I can't speak of it just now. Look at me. I can't even express myself adequately. We have a lot of catching up to do, sir."

"It's 'Father,' not, sir," the Admiral corrected.

"Yes, Father, sir," Laird replied in agreement.

CHAPTER XIV

RESOLUTION COMES TO GRAFTON MANOR

Henry interrupted, "His name isn't' Laird either. Agathe had him baptized Robert Raphaël FitzRoy at St. Andrews by the Wardrobe Church in London."

"If he will accept it, I wish to bestow upon him my title, the Duke of Grafton."

"Milord, I can't even think at the moment. All I want to do is to tell Elizabeth; that's all I can think," Laird remarked as a tear slid down his left cheek.

"I am no longer your lord; I'm your uncle," Henry remarked.

And to that they all raised a glass in unison.

"Should you choose, Her Majesty's Navy has much to offer you as well," the Admiral said.

"Because this is the time for good news, I hope Elizabeth will forgive me for privately announcing our marriage come June. We have been acquainted for eight years—since our childhood. I love her beyond the words to utter," young

Robert announced. "Only, however, please don't share it until we do."

A roar went up as once more, "Hear, hear," resounded.

"A reminder, Robert," Peter interjected, "soon we must take you to see your grandmama as we promised. I'd suggest Elizabeth join us."

"Is it Madam Bancroft to whom you refer?" asked the admiral.

"Yes," answered Peter, "a wonderful lady and actress."

"I saw her this evening but didn't speak. You may think her temperament ladylike, however, had she her way, young Robert wouldn't' be standing here today. Of the many I've known, she alone put the fear of the Almighty in me," the Admiral exclaimed.

Young Robert took note of his remark, with curiosity.

All, including Peter, felt History was moving to a new day, and the anticipation of it excited everyone.

Some day they would learn young Robert was the one who experienced the greater pain from the past, but that would be for another day.

Often that evening young Robert considered he should soon wake, and the day continue on with plain Laird and Elizabeth. Perhaps this was an omen. His excitement in sharing his life with Elizabeth would be reward enough.

But into the next week the dream continued. Peter, Elizabeth, and Robert boarded a coach to Dover and the train station. Three hours later, they stood in Great-Aunt Charlene's apartment, to become acquainted.

"Please, sit by me," insisted Grandmama Bancroft.

She must get her hands on him, she felt.

Taking his arms, staring into his eyes, she confessed, "Yes, you are your mother's boy. Charlene, come see his mother's features. Do you know for whom she named you? Robert, of course, is your father. Raphaël is an archangel with healing in his wings."

Turning to Elizabeth, Madam Bancroft said, "He will be a good man for you. I do wish you both well. I am so moved to live to see this day when all in the world is right."

Charlene moved closer and confirmed the similarities to his mother.

They visited for two hours before Peter interrupted Robert, "We must take our leave to return to Grafton on the train at five."

"Oh... must you go so soon? I have so much to share with you about your mother," Grandmama pleaded as she began sobbing openly, her arms encircling his neck, her tears wetting his collar as well.

"Grandmama, I can't breathe," he whispered. Raising his voice he promised, "We will return soon. Elizabeth and I. I want to know more. Especially I want to learn more of my mother," Robert assured her.

Grandmama loosened her grip, struggling to stand, and clutched Robert as they walked to the door, then released him to go.

"Robert, please don't forget me." she entreated as the four made their way down the corridor.

Reluctantly they continued walking.

Upon leaving the building, Peter handed Squire the signed and witnessed contract of agreement.

He remarked to Peter, "You're a careful man. It has been good working with you. Thank you. You have concluded this just as you promised."

Robert knew he must return before Grandmama passed, and he did. She shared a great wealth of information with him, stories his father might not know or care to tell him.

Hardly a word was spoken as they returned to Grafton Manor.

At his father's behest, young Robert remained on extended leave for more than a month and yet hadn't made up his mind.

His limited life experience could not guide him to the wiser choice. Neither did he appreciate what each path might look like.

Which should he choose, a £100,000, a fortune or personal success? There was no one unbiased to whom to pose his question.

Elizabeth knew of his dilemma, but it didn't occur to him to take her into his confidence. And why not? The results would fall out to her as well.

At their next rendezvous the day following, they discussed it. Elizabeth implied the most important issue was tradition and country. She kindly spoke to Robert, "There's a continual flow of good men to staff the Navy, great people like your father. There is only one of you to advance the

FitzRoy dynasty. Without you, it's certain to fall into disarray and be forgotten. You are nobility, and many will look to you, to us, as examples. We need to honor the Queen, country, and custom. We would do that by carrying on—with tradition."

It made sense to him. Yet, it saddened him to think he would no longer be working with the man he most respected, his father. That he wanted badly.

The four months to June passed so slowly. There was no mistaking the worship they heaped upon one another. They were faithful and chaste to their wedding day.

At noon on June 11th, 1859, the bells tolled at the Knights Templar Church in Dover, the sanctuary filled to overflowing.

From the chancel came the pipe organ music of Wilhelm Richard Wagner's 1850 composition, "The Bridal March," first played at Queen Victoria's eldest daughter's wedding, only months earlier.

Standing with the bishop and Robert's cadre of men, she slowly approached with Jenkins at her arm Robert wore the regalia of the Duke of Grafton, though the title had not yet been conferred upon him officially.

Flowers draped along the aisle with such profusion that the air hung heavy with their pleasant aroma.

The couple knelt facing the bishop and followed in the Lord's Prayer.

The bishop bestowed a prayer of blessing.

"Father, in as much as You have seen fit that these two be joined together, we pray You sustain them and their love for You and for one another. As loved ones and friends, we beseech You to lead them in ways honorable to You and our humble community. Amen."

The couple stood completing their vows, and upon hearing the clergyman's pronouncement kissed one another so passionately the congregation swooned and chuckled with pleasure. Following, they returned to the narthex and from the building. For weeks the community hummed about the most brilliant wedding Dover had ever experienced.

After travel time and nearly two weeks of holiday in Italy, the joyous couple returned home.

Lord Henry's health continued to decline until he was confined to bed.

On young Robert's 20th birthday, with officials of State on hand, the Dukedom was properly conferred upon Robert Raphaël FitzRoy, the seventh Duke of Grafton, and his wife, now Duchess Elizabeth.

Epilogue

Time neither sped up nor slowed down for the family. In 1865 Grandmama, at 84, clung to every visit from Young Robert and Elizabeth. More than anything she was fascinated by the four-year-old twin boys. Robert Raphaël the firstborn, on whose big toe was tied a piece of blue yarn at his birth, and Raphaël Robert. Both sported thick strawberry-colored hair. Her emotions sparkled each time they were present. Although Grandmama wanted her small estate left to them, Robert and Elizabeth shared it with the Hamsteads and their 21 children. Their home had become a well-known institution. Some of their children were grown and on their own. A few worked jobs at the manor.

Lord Henry died on January 10, 1863.

Cecilia enlarged the school, which boasted 27 girls. She had begun a new class: Housekeeping and the Family.' Elizabeth continued to assist her.

Horton was past his prime. Still childless, he had all but adopted Thomas with whom he was very close. He had gained permission to promote Thomas, to his former position as groundskeeper.

Three years earlier, Rupert Brownell, a much younger Hamstead child, had succeeded in becoming a barrister and joined Peter Fenchyl in his practice.

It was never the same for Captain FitzRoy after being promoted to Admiral FitzRoy and assigned to an important administrative post in Her Majesty's Navy. Admiral FitzRoy fell upon serious depression, lasting the final years of his life. He committed suicide in early 1865, in his 59th year. Young Robert struggled for more than two years before finally realizing a degree of closure, appreciative of the time, albeit too short, and the great love they had shared.

The experiment of 'Grafton Forest', due to its success, was duplicated in other far-flung parts of the Kingdom.

In conclusion, the manor lives on. Elizabeth and Robert enjoyed full lives with additional children, grandchildren, and heirs. The New Year's Eve' of Robert's 61st year was special for it moved them all into the anticipated promises of the new century, 1900.

Fidelity and honor were the hallmarks of their lives and the dukedom.

www.ingramcontent.com/pod-product-compliance
Lightning Source LLC
Chambersburg PA
CBHW041012140426
R18136500001B/R181365PG42813CBX00014B/5/J